The Seven Prayers God Always Answers

ALSO BY JASON FRENN

Breaking the Barriers
Power to Reinvent Yourself

Available from FaithWords wherever books are sold.

The Seven Prayers God Always Answers

GOD'S PROMISES FOR EVERYONE,
EVERYWHERE, EVERY TIME

JASON FRENN

New York   Boston   Nashville

FaithWords
Hachette Book Group
1290 Avenue of the Americas
New York, NY 10104

www.faithwords.com

Printed in the United States of America

First Edition: October 2011

14

FaithWords is a division of Hachette Book Group, Inc.
The FaithWords name and logo are trademarks of Hachette Book Group, Inc.

The publisher is not responsible for websites (or their content) that are not owned by the publisher.

Library of Congress Cataloging-in-Publication Data

Frenn, Jason.
  The seven prayers God always answers : God's promises for everyone, everywhere, every time / Jason Frenn.—1st ed.
    p.cm.
  ISBN 978-0-446-54623-2
  1.Prayer—Christianity. I. Title.
  BV220.F46 2011
  248.3'2—dc22
                          2011003836

Dedicated to:
The man who helped me pick the title of this book,
the Cufflink King,
the greatest father a boy could ever ask for,
My Dad

Contents

Acknowledgments

First and foremost, I want to thank the One who answers prayer. Lord, You never leave us nor forsake us. I am eternally grateful for Your unfailing love, concern, and provision over our lives.

Thank you, Cindee, for your patience and love that carried me through the ups and downs of this project. There isn't a day that goes by that I don't thank the Lord for bringing you into my life. Thank you for sharing your story with those who will benefit from reading how you navigated through the turbulent waters. (PS: Write your book!)

Celina, Chanel, and Jazmin, I am the most fortunate father in the world. God has blessed me with three wonderful, God-fearing girls. Thank you for being you.

Dad and Pea Jay, thank you very much for pouring your love into my life. I am grateful for who you are and the example you've become. Dick and Jan (*mis queridos suegros*), thank you for the great story, unwavering faith, and selfless love you show me. Mom, your support over the years has been great. Thank you for letting me know how proud you are.

Thank you, Debbie B., for sharing your story with this vast audience. I know that hundreds of thousands of readers will be impacted by the great things the Lord has done in your life.

Thank you, Jim C., for sitting in the ministry tent and diligently showing the love of Christ to those who would never darken the doors of a local church.

Thank you, Daniel I., for your steadfast commitment to help those whose plight has been long and challenging.

Thank you, Rich Guerra, for being a great leader, a great friend, and a great Christian. I know the reader will enjoy your grandparents' story.

Thank you, Don and Maxine Judkins, for your outstanding commitment to friendship and our mission! The impact of your ministry will be felt for many generations to come!

Thank you, George Wood, for being a great pastor to Cindee and me over the years. You have given so much without asking anything in return. Thank you!

Thank you, Phil Guthrie, Mary Guthrie, Roland Hinz, and all my friends at Radio Nueva Vida. What a gift of God this partnership has been. Your testimony will encourage hundreds of thousands of people!

Thank you, Arturo Alvarado, for your friendship and spiritual support. I couldn't have asked the Lord for a more faithful crusade coordinator during some of the most critical years of crusade ministry.

Thank you, Andrey Romero and Doña Cristina, for your friendship and faithfulness in spite of all the opposition you have faced. I count you among some of my close friends in life.

Thank you, Yolanda Zamorano, for the time you took to share the greatest gift of God with a fifteen-year-old punk kid. It seems as though the seed you sowed fell on good soil. *Gracias por tu fidelidad.*

Thank you, Rolf Zettersten, for taking a chance on this author. Not a day goes by that I don't thank the Lord for allowing me the honor and privilege of working with one of the finest publishers in the world.

Thank you, Joey Paul, for guiding me in this process and being a first-rate editor. In addition to your great skills, you have been a wonderful support to me personally. I am honored to have the opportunity to work with someone of your caliber. (You and Sharon need to write a book too!)

Thank you, Shanon Stowe, for your expertise and professionalism. You have such an encouraging spirit. It's a joy to work with you.

Thank you, Kathleen Stephens, for looking over this document and giving me some great insights before I submitted it. God has gifted you as a wonderful communicator.

Thank you, A. Larry Ross, Kristin Cole, and Steve Yount, for believing in me and for your diligence in helping me get the word out.

Thank you, Zig Ziglar, Tom Ziglar, Julie Norman, Laurie Magers, and all my friends at the Ziglar Corporation. One day a great cloud of witnesses will anxiously await your arrival at The Top!

Thank you, Robert and Arvella Schuller, Sheila and Jim Coleman, Jim and Gretchen Penner, and all my friends at Hour of Power. I am grateful to the Lord for allowing me the opportunity to share behind your pulpit.

Thank you, Lori Class, Carrie Paterson, Cindy Surch, Erica Davis, Socorro Dimacali, Joe Class, Lori Schubert,

Kimberly Connelly, Leah Yingling, Nancy Infante, Natalie McBroom, Vicki Tewalt, Ron Henry, Shirley Alexander, Scott Anderson, Stacy Holmes, Susan Thibault, and Steve Harrison for taking time to read the manuscript and give me your valuable feedback. Finally, thank you Sharon Paul for praying for me as I wrote this book!

What Do You Want Me to Do for You?

W hat prayer do you want answered? If you could sit down with God over a cup of coffee and He asked you, "What do you want Me to do for you?"—what would you say? What would you ask? Think about it. His question could usher in the greatest breakthrough of your life. I believe that God answers prayer. Yes, even yours.

While it's true that God is not a genie, nor is He Santa Claus, He nonetheless wants to "give you the desires of your heart" (Ps. 37:4 NKJV). He understands your needs, and with a heart filled with love, generosity, and compassion, He reaches out to you at this time in your life.

Over the years, people have asked me some very interesting questions about prayer. Quite often they ask, "Is it unspiritual to ask God to help me get out of debt or make more money?" On occasion, some have quietly inquired if it's all right to pray for a more dynamic and meaningful sex life in their marriage. One person asked me if God cared enough to hear her petition to be a better tennis player. While these prayer requests might seem unimportant to some, to those who are searching for answers, they are very important. In almost every situation my response is the same. God cares more than you think, and yes, you should share your heart with the Lord. There is hardly a conversation with God you shouldn't have, especially if your heart is genuine and your desire is sincere. The following story illustrates just how much God cares about the details of our lives.

"God, we need Your help. We need Your provision." Those were the sincere words I jotted down on a piece of paper sitting in a mandatory meeting just before the noon hour. My wife, girls, and I were planning to return to the United States from Central America for a year of itineration (traveling across the country to raise our ministerial budget). We needed no less than $5,000 for travel, a down payment on a used vehicle, security deposit, and first month's rent, and if anything was left over, clothes for the girls. In short, we needed a financial miracle. That was March 31, 1999. April came and went. Our departure date was May 24.

The last weekend we were in Costa Rica, I spoke at a church called Oasis of Hope. I remember that night vividly. Because we were so strapped for cash, my shoes had holes in the soles. One of the ushers in the church came up to me and said, "Jason, would it bother you if I cleaned up your shoes? It's just that they are too dirty." Although it was a bit humiliating, I sat down in the back of the sanctuary while she polished them. Afterward, I thanked her, and she returned to her post.

That night, I shared a simple message of how God is the God of second chances. When I finished, the associate pastor walked onto the platform and, unbeknownst to me, announced that the church was going to receive an offering for us. Afterward, he instructed me to use it however I saw fit. The offering was $1,000. We were overwhelmed with gratitude for their generosity, and we were grateful, of course, to the Lord.

The week prior to our departure, we still needed $4,000. That was when I received a call from my father-in-law asking if I would be interested in translating for an Argentine evangelist at a crusade in San Diego, California, scheduled the day after we arrived. The coordinators needed someone to interpret from Spanish to English. I felt honored by the invitation and told him that I would be glad to help.

Five days later, we landed in Southern California and headed to the crusade. Along the way we stopped at a shopping mall to purchase new shoes. I didn't want people to see my toes pushing through the soles.

The crusade went well.

The following morning, both the preacher and I were invited to eat breakfast with the pastors who had sponsored the event. I took all three of our girls to the restaurant while Cindee enjoyed some peace and quiet in the room. After we finished eating, the coordinator said, "Thank you so much for serving us in this capacity. You have truly blessed our hearts." After giving an envelope to the speaker, he turned and gave one to me as well. I assumed that it was an offering for serving as the interpreter. I asked if I could apply whatever was in the envelope to any particular need we had. He replied, "Of course."

After saying good-bye and exchanging hugs, I said to the girls, "Come on. Let's go for a walk on the beach and find a park." They were excited.

I waited until we found a set of swings and a jungle gym before I pulled out the envelope. The girls immediately started climbing like monkeys turned loose in a tree. I opened the envelope thinking, *There's probably a check for $250 to $300.* I unfolded the check. At first, my eyes couldn't believe it. *This can't be right,* I thought. The dollar amount read "$4,000.00." I rubbed my eyes for a second to ensure that my vision was clear. Then I focused on the portion where the check writer spelled out the amount on the check. It read: "Four thousand dollars and _____ xx/100."

I jumped up and screamed, "Hallelujah. God is our provider!" Indeed, He is our provider. As I danced around that little park my girls wondered what had gotten into me. In one powerful blow, God erased every financial need we had. There was enough money for us to purchase a used vehicle, set up an apartment, and buy some clothes for the entire family. I was so excited.

Six weeks later, we embarked upon the itineration trail. We were driving from California to Tennessee and spent the night in a hotel in New Mexico. Sitting on the side of the bed in the late afternoon, I received a call on my cell phone.

The voice on the other end was very serious. A man asked, "Is this Jason Frenn?"

I said, "Yes."

He said, "I believe you translated for a recent crusade in the San Diego area. I am the accountant for the outreach. By chance when you received a check from us, was it made out for the amount of $400?"

It felt like the world's rotation came to a grinding halt.

I took a deep breath and said, "No! No! The check you gave me was for the amount of $4,000."

He said, "Four thousand dollars?! Well, that's where all the money went. There has been a huge mistake, a $3,600 mistake to be exact! We need to resolve this problem. I have no idea what I was thinking. How's your financial situation? Perhaps we can work out a solution."

In about seven seconds, I told him the entire story, from my journal entry to the moment when he called me that afternoon.

After I explained everything that happened, I said, "Now, if you are saying that the check amount was a mistake and that we need to give you back $3,600, I am going to need a little bit of time. Because that four grand is *gone*!"

There was a long pause.

"If you're telling me that you needed exactly $4,000, I can only assume the Lord led me to write out a check for that exact amount. It must be God's will. Keep the $4,000. I'll figure out how I will manage things on my end. God bless you!"

Then he hung up.

Indeed, God answered my request. Through a series of unpredictable circumstances, His provision came at the moment when we needed it. Never too early, never too late, His timing is always impeccable.

It's been nearly twelve years, and we have seen hundreds upon hundreds of prayers answered. God has never abandoned us, never misled us, nor given us false hopes. He has seen us through thick and thin.

What about you? What are your dreams, aspirations, and desires? What mountain are you facing? What prayer do you want answered?

What This Book Can Do for You

In preparation for writing this book, I surveyed more than one thousand people and asked them one question: "If you could ask God in prayer for three things knowing that He would answer your request, what would you ask?" The answers were intriguing.

The single greatest prayer request was for the *spiritual salvation* of a family member or friend. The second-largest request was for some sort of *financial breakthrough* or *career advancement*. The third was for *physical healing*, often for someone else. The fourth was for *spiritual growth*. The fifth most popular prayer request was for *physical protection and safety for their children, families*, or *themselves*. Finally, people wanted the strength and opportunity to *fulfill God's call* upon their lives.

Odds are, the prayers you want God to answer fall into one of the areas mentioned above, and my desire is that this book will help you pray and see the results that you desire. I pray that you see a major breakthrough, not in one area of your life but in many. I believe that it is God's intent to help you move beyond the obstacles that keep you or a loved one from moving forward.

This book will give you insight into the prayers that God always answers. It will teach you to understand His heart so that you can pray in accordance with His will. This book will build your faith to move mountains. It will help you experience His power. My desire is that this book completely transforms your life!

Ask for the Impossible!

A man born blind was sitting along the side of the road. Each day, he held out his hand, hoping that those who passed by would drop a few coins into his cup. One day, he heard a distant rumble caused by a rather large entourage heading his way. Up until that time, no one born blind had ever recovered his or her sight (John 9:32). When he asked the person standing next to him what all the commotion was about, his neighbor replied, "Jesus of Nazareth is passing by."

The famous healer has come to my town, he thought. Waiting for the precise moment when the central figure of the parade was at the shortest distance, he raised his voice and said, "Jesus, Son of David, have mercy on me!" Those close by rebuked him and told him not to bother the Master. But he raised his voice even louder. That's when Christ stopped, turned to His disciples, and said, "Bring him!" They brought him before the healer. Jesus asked him the question that sooner or later He asks every one of us: "What do you want Me to do for you?"

At that moment, the beggar could have answered, "I'd like a million dollars," or perhaps "I'd like to be super famous." Instead, he asked for the only thing that had never been done in the history of the world. He asked for what seemed to be impossible. "I want to see," he said. Without hesitating, Christ granted his request, saying, "Your faith has healed you." (Story paraphrased from Luke 18:35–42 NIV.)

Just like those who tried to discourage the beggar, there will always be people who feel it's their duty to tell you how insignificant you are. There will always be people who tell you that you don't matter, especially when your dreams seem impossible. There will always be people who have the gift of raining on your parade. But God won't. He cares about you. He always listens, because He loves you. So ask Him for what's never been done before in your life. I challenge you to ask Him for the impossible.

As a missionary evangelist who has served throughout Latin America, the Caribbean, and the United States, my experience is that God answers the prayers placed within the pages of this book. I write from the experience of someone who lived fifteen years in the heart of Central America and has seen God transform the lives of hundreds of thousands of people. Without a doubt, He is interested in the details of your life. Ultimately, friend, it's your faith placed in Him that will allow you to see the miracles and the breakthrough you seek.

Our Road Map

This book is about seven prayers that God always answers. These are prayers that aim to motivate the hand of God to direct you, forgive you, free you, provide for you, heal you, bless you, and save you. They are biblical, and I carry a deep conviction that they were born in God's heart to benefit and bless your life. It's fair to say that God answers all prayer with a "yes," "no," or "wait." However the prayers discussed in this book all have something wonderful in common. They are prayers to which God always responds positively in one way or another. In a day when people question whether God interacts with humanity and when unbelief is spreading like a virus, this book aims to teach you to pray in such a way that you clearly see the hand of God move powerfully.

This book can serve you in two ways. First, you can apply these prayers to your personal life. Or if you are a leader, you can also apply them corporately to those you currently serve or lead, such as your family, church, or organization.

Each chapter is dedicated to a prayer. Beginning with chapter 1, the chapters are divided into sections that will explain each prayer, lay a biblical foundation, provide powerful testimonies, give different examples regarding how you might implement the specific type of prayer in your life, and teach you to pray in a way that helps you see results in each of the given areas.

As we conclude this introduction, I want to focus your attention on the first question we talked about earlier. I believe that God asks you the same question at this time in your life. At the beginning of this chapter, I gave you a scenario. If you could sit down over a cup of coffee with the Lord and He asked you, "What do you want Me to do for you?" what would be your answer?

As we begin this journey together, I am going to ask you to be mindful of two things. First, make a mental note of the prayers you want God to answer. Second, keep your eyes open to the possible ways He may use to answer them. (Please see Instructions for a Prayer Journal located at the end of the book.)

If you desire to see your prayers answered, fasten your seat belt and prepare yourself for some incredible and miraculous things to happen in your life. If you're ready to experience something transformational, turn the page, and we'll begin that journey together!

The Seven Prayers God Always Answers

CHAPTER ONE

The Prayer for Direction

A friend of mine who pastors in a large US city recently told me about a middle-aged man in his church. I'll call him John. My colleague was leading a midweek Bible study covering how God guided and spoke to people in the Old Testament. One night after they adjourned, John headed for his car. He paused for a moment and prayed, "God, please direct me and speak to me like you did in the Old Testament. I want to recognize Your voice and direction." Then he started his vehicle and headed home. As he drove down the road, he felt an impression telling him to go into a store to make a purchase. *That's strange*, he thought. *It must be my imagination.* He tried to dismiss it, but the impression grew.

As John approached a convenience store, he sensed that he should go inside and purchase some milk. He struggled to discern whether it was the Lord or something he was conjuring up in his head. He parked and went inside. After walking down a couple of aisles, he found himself

1

standing in front of the refrigerated section. *Okay, this is really strange*, he thought. *I am just about to buy some milk without any logical explanation.* "But God," he muttered, "I don't even drink the stuff." Nonetheless, there was a consistent conviction that insisted buying the milk was the right thing to do. Feeling somewhat conflicted, he grabbed a gallon, paid the cashier, and drove down the street. His adventure was just about to become even more peculiar.

As he approached a low-income neighborhood notorious for its high crime, he suddenly felt another impression: *Turn right. You've got to be kidding me*, he thought. *Is this real?* The sense didn't fade away. Instead, it grew. "Fine," he said. "If it's You, Lord, I need You to guide me through this." Finally, after a couple of turns, he felt the Lord saying to him, "That's the house." The street was dark due to the fact that two of the streetlights were burned out. He slowed down, pulled alongside the curb, and parked his vehicle in front of the residence. The still, small voice said, "Go up to that house, ring the doorbell, and give them the milk." John took a deep breath as a futile attempt to overcome the fear of embarrassment and headed to the front door.

As soon as he got out of his car, the neighbor's dog started to bark through the chain-link fence in the backyard. Heading up to the house, he noticed the uncut grass and the driveway filled with patches of asphalt. He stepped onto the porch and rang the doorbell, but at first no one answered. After waiting a minute, he rang it again. Finally, someone cracked open the door. It was a young Hispanic man.

John said, "Listen, I know this sounds completely crazy, but I purchased this gallon of milk, and I believe I am supposed to give it to you." Without saying a word, the man grabbed the milk and ran down the hallway, raising his voice in Spanish. After a few moments, a young woman came to the door with a baby in her arms. With broken English and tears streaming down her face she said, "My husband and I could only afford to buy a few grocery items, and we didn't have enough money for milk for our twelve-month-old baby. Tonight before you came, we prayed that the Lord would send an angel to help us. Then you rang the doorbell. By chance are you an angel?"

Whether you seek God's guidance during the most critical moment of your life or you feel stuck in a rut, this chapter aims to help you pray more effectively by providing sound biblical principles and examples and real-world testimonies. It is divided into three sections. The first lays a biblical foundation for the prayer for direction. The second section shows how the prayer for direction can profoundly impact five specific areas of your life. The third section offers direction when you feel uncertain and overwhelmed in your time of need. As we begin, let's establish a biblical foundation in regard to the first prayer that God always answers: *the prayer for direction.*

I. Biblical Examples of God Answering the Prayer for Direction

The Bible refers to God's direction for those who seek it more than twenty-five times in both the Old and the New Testaments. I've listed a few verses to help you understand the way God responds to those who seek Him:

By day the LORD went ahead of them in a pillar of cloud to guide them on their way and by night in a pillar of fire to give them light, so that they could travel by day or night. (Exodus 13:21)

The Israelites went up and wept before the LORD until evening, and they inquired of the LORD. They said, "Shall we go up again to battle against the Benjamites, our brothers?" The LORD answered, "Go up against them." (Judges 20:23)

When David was told, "Look, the Philistines are fighting against Keilah and are looting the threshing floors," he inquired of the LORD, saying, "Shall I go and attack these Philistines?" The LORD answered him, "Go, attack the Philistines and save Keilah." (1 Samuel 23:1–2)

David inquired of the LORD, "Shall I pursue this raiding party? Will I overtake them?" "Pursue them," he answered. "You will certainly overtake them and succeed in the rescue." (1 Samuel 30:8)

He sought God during the days of Zechariah, who instructed him in the fear of God. As long as he sought the LORD, God gave him success. (2 Chronicles 26:5)

The LORD directs the steps of the godly. He delights in every detail of their lives. (Psalm 37:23 NLT)

When he, the Spirit of truth, comes, he will guide you into all truth. He will not speak on his own; he will speak only what he hears, and he will tell you what is yet to come. (John 16:13)

In addition to these verses that talk about incidents where God answered prayers for direction, there are two incidents where God did not answer such requests. In both cases, the person was not sincere. Because of his disingenuous heart and openness to the occult, God regretted ever placing this person in leadership (1 Sam. 15:11). His name was King Saul.

> Saul asked God, "Shall I go down after the Philistines? Will you give them into Israel's hand?" But God did not answer him that day. (1 Samuel 14:37)

> When Saul saw the Philistine army, he was afraid; terror filled his heart. He inquired of the LORD, but the LORD did not answer him by dreams or Urim or prophets. Saul then said to his attendants, "Find me a woman who is a medium, so I may go and inquire of her." (1 Samuel 28:5–7)

There is a biblical explanation why God did not respond to Saul's request: "Saul died because he was unfaithful to the LORD; he did not keep the word of the LORD and even consulted a medium for guidance, and did not inquire of the LORD. So the LORD put him to death and turned the kingdom over to David son of Jesse" (1 Chron. 10:13–14).

So then, besides faith, what is the prerequisite to God's answering our prayers? Is it perfect theology? Not necessarily. The Bible has many examples of people who had misconceptions or erroneous ideas, but God nonetheless chose to bless and heal them (Mark 9:39–40; Luke 9:49–50). Is the prerequisite a perfect heart? Probably not. How many times did David sin, spill innocent blood, or lie to save his own neck? Yet in spite of his actions, God blessed him and answered his prayers. So what is the prerequisite? It's a genuine heart. When you pray with sincerity, God responds. As long as you don't have a heart like Saul's, you can be confident that He will respond when you ask Him for direction.

Are you looking for guidance? If so, I have researched the prayers that God always answers, and the first one I want to share with you is the *prayer for direction*. In the case of those who have genuine and sincere hearts, I have never encountered a place in Scripture where God did not respond favorably to their requests. The prayer outlined below is biblical. Many great men and women of faith have prayed a similar prayer. If you need direction, pray this prayer or read it and put it in your own words as you begin and end your day. Then use the example of the prayer journal in the back of the book to record how God answers.

The Prayer for Direction

God, You order the steps of a righteous person. If I have found favor in Your eyes, guide every step I take and guide every action. Help me to recognize Your path and discern where You want me to go. Open doors no one can shut, and shut every door I should avoid. Allow me to see clearly your direction without any confusion. Give me a clear sign today, this week, or this month regarding the direction I should take. I want to do Your will. Guide me in Christ's name, amen.

Although you can apply this prayer to many different areas in your life, you may feel the need for guidance in something specific. For that reason, I have outlined five distinct areas that offer godly insights on prayer for God's guidance and direction. They include God's guidance for general direction, relationships, finances, health, and family.

II. How the Prayer for Direction Can Transform Five Areas of Your Life

1. Discovering God's Direction for Your Life

Have you ever asked yourself, *What am I doing with my life?* I know I have a time or two. Many times we can become irritated when we don't seem to be headed in the right direction. During times of frustration, we may feel like we are going in circles or simply living in survival mode, or existing from one day to the next. It's during those times, if we are open, God will lead us. In spite of our circumstances, God responds to our requests for direction and helps point us toward godly solutions.

Imagine being seventy-five years old and feeling restless because your life hasn't turned out the way you envisioned. Let's say that you tried to have kids, but you and your wife were unsuccessful. To make matters worse, you were planning to move to a wonderful place for retirement, but because of circumstances beyond your control you were forced to stop five hundred miles short of your goal. This scenario is not fiction. It was Abraham's life. He probably felt frustrated from time to time.

When Abraham sought God's direction, the Lord responded, "Leave your country, your people and your father's household and go to the land I will show you. I will make you into a great nation and I will bless you; I will make your name great, and you will be a blessing. I will bless those who bless you, and whoever curses you I will curse; and all peoples on earth will be blessed through you" (Gen. 12:1–3).

So Abraham set out as the Lord directed him. He had a new lease on life, and God guided him every step of the way. What was the end result? He and his family inherited the Promised Land. "By faith Abraham, when called to go to a place he would later receive as his inheritance, obeyed and went, even though he did not know where he was going. By faith he made his home in the promised land like a stranger in a foreign country; he lived in tents, as did Isaac and Jacob, who were heirs with him of the same promise" (Heb. 11:8–9).

When you ask God for direction, you will receive it; if you seek answers, He promises that you will find them; if you are looking for a door, He says the right one will open for you (Luke 11:9). If you struggle with the question "What am I doing with my life?" the Lord will speak to you and give you direction.

Like most immigrants, Felipe came to the United States in search of a better life. His hope and dream was to start over, build wealth, and raise his family in a world of opportunity. Unfortunately, shortly after their arrival in the San Fernando Valley, he started to drink. Soon his daily habit turned into a vice. His wife, Juana, worked hard to keep the family afloat.

One day, she was walking down the street and saw

what she thought was a circus tent. Somewhat curious, she walked through the vinyl curtains expecting to see clowns, a trapeze, and an assortment of wild animals. To her bewilderment, it wasn't a circus. It was an evangelistic campaign. She didn't want to leave abruptly. So she sat down in the back and waited for an opportune moment to slip out. The service began, and before she knew it, she was listening to the message.

The preacher said, "Jesus Christ can forgive your sins. Give your life to Him today!" When he gave the invitation, Juana got up and walked to the front and gave her life to the Lord. Something miraculous took place. The burden she had carried for years was suddenly lifted. As she walked home that night, she pondered the reason her family had come to the United States. They came for a better life, and God guided them every step of the way.

When she returned home, her husband, fairly inebriated, was waiting for her. He said, "Where have you been?" She said, "I went to the tent meeting three blocks from here. It's not a circus. It's a church."

"What?!" exclaimed Felipe. "You went to a religious service?"

"Yes, I did."

"Well, I forbid you to go back ever again," he said. "As a matter of fact, if you ever go back, I am going to take my gun, shoot the preacher, and drag you out by your hair in front of everyone! Do you understand me?!"

Being a strong Latin woman, she wasn't about to be told what she could or couldn't do. Besides, she believed that God was directing her steps, and she knew that the very best thing for her family was to follow God's leading. She purposed in her heart to go the next night.

Late the next afternoon, she headed to the campaign. When her husband found out where she had gone, he grabbed his gun and tucked it into the back of his pants underneath his jacket. He said to himself, *When I get there, I'm going to shoot that preacher and drag my wife out of that meeting by her hair in front of everyone. She'll regret going against my word.* Then in his drunken, angry state, he set out for the campaign.

As he left the house, it started to rain. By the time he reached the tent, it was pouring. He quickly slipped into the back and stood for a few moments. He wanted to wait until it stopped raining before making his move. But the rain never let up, and he finally sat down. During his message, the pastor repeated the phrase he had used the night before: "Jesus Christ can forgive your sins. Give your life to Him today!" Tears began to run down Felipe's cheeks. The one question that ran through his mind was, *What am I doing with my life?*

When the pastor gave the invitation, Felipe stood to his feet and walked to the front. That night Felipe Guerra gave his heart to the Lord and began a lifelong journey that impacted generations to come. Both he and his wife came to this country in search of a better life, and through a series of unforeseen events, they found it. God helped them find the answer to the question "What am I doing with my life?"

A few years later, Felipe Guerra started one of the first Spanish-speaking Pentecostal churches in the San Fernando Valley, and in 1960, his five-year-old grandson, Rich, gave his life to Christ in a service in that church plant. Today, Rich Guerra is the superintendent of the Assemblies of God in Southern California. God leads people just like Abraham and Felipe every day. And He blesses the generations that follow them.

Will He answer your prayer for direction? Absolutely! The following prayer will help you ask for God's guidance for general direction so that you will see His mighty hand move in your life:

> God, I ask You to give me clear direction and guidance for my life and in my current circumstances. Sometimes I feel disillusioned and disappointed. Show me Your path that will bring blessing to my life, my family, and my other relationships. I believe You have a specific purpose and destiny for me. Help me to identify it and give me the strength to walk in harmony with Your divine will. Give me the eyes to see your direction clearly without any distraction or confusion. I ask this in Christ's name, amen.

2. Discovering God's Direction for Your Relationships

Wouldn't you like to know which relationships are truly worth the investment? How many people make friends with individuals who have no sense of commitment or faithfulness? Or worse, how many friendships bring out the worst in people by tearing them down instead of lifting them up? How many women become disillusioned over a relationship that goes nowhere or hold onto a guy that has never truly grown up? And in the business world, how many good-hearted people find out after it's too late that their business partner embezzled from them?

God can guide you toward the friendships that are healthy and steer you away from the ones that are destructive. How? When you ask Him to lead you in regard to the relationships in your life, whether they are professional or casual, He will freely give you the insight you need. Perhaps one of the best examples of a godly relationship is the one between David and Jonathan. It was a friendship guided by the Lord.

The young man looked down upon the unconscious giant. The soldiers came out of hiding and began to cheer the young sheep herder. He then took Goliath's sword, lifted it high in the air, and decapitated him. After killing Goliath, David became an instant national celebrity. However, King Saul wasn't impressed. He became jealous that the Lord's favor was upon him. Eventually, his jealousy grew to fear, and his fear turned to hatred. Many times he conspired to kill David, but the king's son, Jonathan, intervened. No matter how elaborate the plan, Jonathan managed to get a message to his friend in order to save his life.

Jonathan was next in line to inherit the throne, but as long as David was alive, his becoming king was in question. Even so, he never thought twice about his commitment to David. He never put his own career ahead of his friend.

Jonathan went so far as to meet in secret with David when he was deeply distressed and "helped him find strength in God. 'Don't be afraid,' he said. 'My father Saul will not lay a hand on you. You will be king over Israel, and I will be second to you. Even my father Saul knows this'"(1 Sam. 23:16–18). How did David find such a devout friend? David was someone who asked God to lead him. He constantly prayed. That's why the Lord guided David in the choices he made regarding his relationships. He directed David and Jonathan's relationship. When we ask God for direction, He helps us pick and develop our relationships. He offers guidance when we are willing to follow His lead.

Take a moment and ask yourself the following question: *Do I have a godly friend in my life like Jonathan, someone who would risk so much for me? Do my friends lift me up or tear me down?* Believe me, friend, God wants you to live a fruitful and meaningful life. He wants to guide you toward the relationships that will lift you up and bring out the very best in you.

Soon after I began my relationship with Christ, I realized that I needed to grow spiritually, but my old friends didn't share my new spiritual convictions. I asked the Lord to help me develop godly relationships and discern which ones were worth the investment, which ones would be fruitful, and which ones would be healthy. Up until that point, most of my friendships revolved around sports, parties, and arcades. It wasn't long until the Lord brought someone into my life who encouraged me and lifted me up. He invited me to join him for times of prayer and Bible study. I prayed, and God placed someone in my life during a time when I needed a good friend.

The same can be said about my wife. I prayed for years for the right person to marry. Although I dated a couple of wonderful people, the person God guided into my life is one of the finest I know. She is someone of deep moral character, integrity, trust, and, most important, spiritual depth. Of all the human relationships we can have, the one with a spouse is arguably the most important. If you sincerely seek His direction, God will guide you to meet and develop godly friendships and relationships with people who will be a great blessing to you.

If your current relationships are not uplifting, if they bring out the worst in you, if they move you in the wrong direction, then I highly recommend that you ask God to guide you. Perhaps God will lead you in such a way that you are able to transform and enrich the relationships that are important to you. Or perhaps He will confirm that it's time to move on. In either case, if you seek Him, He will guide your steps. That's a promise you can count on (Prov. 20:24).

God directs people every day, and I have no doubt that He will answer your prayer for direction regarding your relationships. The prayer below comes from several Biblical sources that you can use as an example for asking God to guide you in your relationships. If you need God's direction for the relationships in your life, I would encourage you to pray this prayer or one that comes from your heart every day. Then make a note of the changes that take place.

Lord, help me to become a good and godly friend to those in my life, and help me to identify and cultivate the godly friendships that will pick me up instead of tear me down. Guide me to find friends who will bring out the best in me and encourage me to grow closer to You. Give me the strength to move away from the relationships that are not fruitful and closer to the ones that are. I ask You to guide all my personal and professional relationships. In Christ's name I pray, amen.

3. Discovering God's Direction for Your Finances

As of January 2010, the US had more than 576 million credit cards in circulation, and the average American family had $15,519 in credit card debt. The total U.S. consumer debt was $2.44 trillion, and the U.S. credit card default rate was 11.17 percent.[1] As I write this book, I feel deeply compelled to urge you to seek God's direction in regard to your finances.

As someone who started his professional career in sales before becoming a missionary, I realized early on that, regardless of one's occupation, prayer for God's direction is the starting point. It is essential, especially when dealing with our finances. How can I make that statement? God never leads anyone into financial ruin. He never leads people into more debt than they should take on.

When Cindee and I got married, we financed our wedding. We financed our furniture. We financed the honeymoon. At the time, we both made a good salary. I worked as a sales representative for a Fortune 500 company, and she worked as an executive assistant for a mergers and acquisitions corporation. Like most, we justified our expenditures. However, after four months we realized that we were not eliminating our debt as swiftly as we'd planned. We were barely making our minimum payments.

Our plan was to move to Costa Rica as missionaries two years later, but our missions organization wouldn't accept applications from individuals with as much debt as we had. Cindee and I prayed a simple prayer: "God, we're in a hole. Please help us get out!" I was hoping that God would have opened the floodgates of heaven and poured out an avalanche of dough upon our lives. God responded. But it wasn't the response I was looking for. Instead of sending someone with an anonymous envelope containing a winning lottery ticket or an uncle who left me an inheritance, the Lord issued a direct and clear word: "Sell all your new furniture, move out of your new apartment, move into a trailer, and buy your replacement furniture at garage sales."

"What?" I asked. "But we have a baby coming in four months." The Lord said, "If you want to get your financial house in order, you have to make wise choices, as painful as they may seem."

Please don't misunderstand me. This is not financial advice. This is spiritual advice. We wanted to be free, and we wanted to move to the mission field. So we did everything the Lord led us to do. In twelve months our debt dropped from more than $23,000 to $2,500. Was there ever a windfall of money? No. Did God guide us financially? Absolutely. Was it difficult? For the first two months. Were we ever in danger? Never!

In the Bible, God never turned His back on those whose hearts were sincere and genuine and who sought His guidance. "'Let us build up these towns,' [King Asa] said to Judah, 'and put walls around them, with towers, gates and bars. The land is still ours, because we have sought the LORD our God; we sought him and he has given us rest on every side.' So they built and prospered" (2 Chron. 14:7).

"This is what Hezekiah did throughout Judah, doing what was good and right and faithful before the LORD his God. In everything that he undertook in the service of God's temple and in obedience to the law and the commands, he sought his God and worked wholeheartedly. And so he prospered" (2 Chron. 31:20–21).

"Jabez cried out to the God of Israel, 'Oh, that you would bless me and enlarge my territory! Let your hand be with me, and keep me from harm so that I will be free from pain.' And God granted his request" (1 Chron. 4:9).

Finally, this is what God says to those who are unequivocally willing to follow His lead when it comes to their finances: "'Test me in this,' says the LORD Almighty, 'and see if I will not throw open the floodgates of heaven and pour out so much blessing that you will not have room enough for it'" (Mal. 3:10).

If you've come to the point where you recognize the need for God's guidance regarding your finances, I believe He will graciously impart to you His infinite wisdom and insight. He will answer your prayer for financial direction. If you feel the need to have a simple prayer that can help you begin, consider the following prayer as an example:

> Lord, I realize that money is not everything, but it is necessary for the things I need. I want You to trust me financially. Show me what I must do to become a great steward. Guide my steps so that my family and I can walk in Your blessings and provision. Help me to resist all the temptations that keep me from moving forward. I ask You to lead me in Christ's name, amen.

4. Discovering God's Direction for Your Health

Of all the prayer requests that flow across the Internet, by far the largest category pertains to physical health. Every day I receive more than twenty requests in my personal e-mail box from people all over the world asking for God's intervention. To me, it's very interesting. Jesus set out to help people physically, and today that need is just as viable as ever. After centuries of medical advancement, people still need God's help for physical remedies. We become ill, die prematurely, and still battle diseases that have plagued humanity for millennia. As we see in the following story, Naaman was a powerful leader who had no other options but to follow God's direction.

He was a highly respected military commander in the army of the king of Aram. Although he was successful on many battlefronts, he was losing his personal battle against leprosy.

An Israelite girl who wound up working in his home as a maidservant said to him, "If only my master would see the prophet who is in Samaria! He would cure him of his leprosy" (2 Kings 5:3). When Naaman asked his superior if he could go to Samaria, he not only agreed, but he also sent a letter to the king of Israel that read, "With this letter I am sending my servant Naaman to you so that you may cure him of his leprosy" (5:6).

At first the king of Israel was disturbed because he felt personally responsible for the man's cure. When the prophet Elisha heard about it, though, he immediately realized it was an opportunity to glorify the Lord. He sent word to the king saying, "Why are you so upset? Have the man come to me and he will know that there is a prophet in Israel" (5:8).

Naaman went to Elisha's door, but instead of coming out to greet him, Elisha sent a message to him that said, "Go, wash yourself seven times in the Jordan, and your flesh will be restored and you will be cleansed" (5:10). When Naaman heard the message and realized that Elisha was not coming out, he was furious. He said to his servants, "I thought that he would surely come out to me and stand and call on the name of the LORD his God, wave his hand over the spot and cure me of my leprosy" (5:11). In his mind, there were plenty of rivers in his own country. He couldn't see what was so special about the Jordan.

Finally, several of his servants said to him, "My father,

if the prophet had told you to do some great thing, would you not have done it? How much more, then, when he tells you, 'Wash and be cleansed'!" (5:13). Naaman let go of his pride and washed himself in the Jordan. When he emerged after dipping in the river seven times, his skin was like that of a young boy. The leprosy was completely gone.

The great commander returned to Elisha's house, this time humbled by the miracle God had done. He confessed that there was no God in all of creation like the God of Israel. He wanted to give Elisha gifts, but he refused. Elisha worked for the Lord, and the compensation that God gave him was more than enough.

Naaman was a man of integrity. Through the word of a young girl, God led him to a place where his health could be restored. Even when he was ready to walk away from the gift of God, the Lord directed the words of his servants to convince him to turn around and head back to the Jordan. It was God's course of action. It was precisely the direction that Naaman needed.

Many people today face similar circumstances. When I ask people in cities throughout the United States, Latin America, and the Caribbean what their greatest prayer requests are, many indicate that they need God's help to face the problems that are affecting their bodies. Many times, unfortunately, the medical community has no solution. That's when we need God to lead us. And if we turn to Him, He will guide us and help us find the answers.

I believe that God works on every front to bring healing and restoration to the human race. Whether the man of God "waves his hand over the spot and cures you of your leprosy" or a chemist discovers a new form of cancer treatment in a laboratory, I believe both are God-inspired. Both are victories, and both are examples of the power of God. Let me explain.

I went to the post office on Monday morning to pick up our medical clearance forms. At the time, I was twenty-three years old. Everything looked good except one number pertaining to my blood work. My cholesterol was 297. *That's impossible*, I said to myself. The doctor's note read, "Try a low cholesterol diet, and recheck in two months."

I bought a book on lowering cholesterol, ran every morning, and took all the right vitamins. After two months, I lost twenty pounds and went in for my blood work. My cholesterol dropped more than 120 points. *That's that*, I thought. *All I have to do is eat right and exercise, and I won't have to worry about it again.*

Eight years later, our mission organization sent us in for complete physicals. This time my cholesterol was 250, and my blood pressure was 140 over 85. Heart disease runs in my family. So naturally, I became concerned. Although I hadn't gained any weight, it seemed as though my genes were taking over.

I must have asked a hundred people to pray for me. I would have preferred that God heal me instantly, but unfortunately, that did not happen.

I will never forget going in for my physical when I was thirty-eight. The doctor unwrapped the cuff from my arm and asked, "How do you feel?" I said, "I feel fine. Why?" He said, "Your blood pressure is 170 over 100. Are you sure you feel fine?" I said, "Well, now that you mention it, since I started talking with you, I feel pretty lousy." I was frustrated, to say the least. In the years leading up to that moment, I had worked extremely hard to get in shape and eat right, and what did I have to show for it? After all those years of putting off gratification, I still had to take medication. Then he sat down and took a look at my blood work. That's when he dropped the second bombshell: "Your cholesterol is 272. I recommend you take medication for that, too."

When I left his office, I went home and prayed. I said, "God, I would have preferred that You heal my body. For some reason, You chose not to do so. Please guide me. Speak to me. Give me a sign of the best course of action. I really don't want to take medication, because I am relatively young, but then again, I don't want to make my wife a widow either. I ask You to guide me during this hour of decision."

I spoke with two other doctors, one in Springfield, Missouri, the other in Newport Beach, California. They both confirmed that the medication I was prescribed in Costa Rica was the right one for me. The most convincing conversation, however, was the one I had with God. One morning while I was jogging, I felt an overwhelming impression that changed the way I look at how God leads people in regard to their health. He said to me, "Jason, why don't you take the medication? I have engineered your body to work with it so you can experience a decent quality of life. Regardless if I heal you at an altar or you take medication, you still need a miracle. You still need your body's chemistry to function with medication. Every human body is different. In essence, everyone needs some sort of miracle, including you. This is your miracle." Like Naaman, I had to swallow my pride in order to do what God instructed me to do. I reluctantly followed God's direction, and He gave me a wonderful gift as a result. Today, my health is great. My blood pressure and cholesterol are very low, thanks to the miracles that God has inspired in the medical community.

God gladly gives guidance to those who seek Him. He answers the prayer for direction by speaking to you directly or by placing people in your life who will provide godly wisdom.

Perhaps you've come to a point where you need God's help regarding your health. Maybe you're frustrated because no matter whom you talk to, you can't seem to get any answers. I believe that as you seek, God will provide an open door. He will provide the answers when no one else can. Turn your heart to Him in your time of physical need, and He will guide you. Perhaps you might consider praying the following prayer:

Lord, my body is not responding as I hoped, but I recognize that You are the Author and Finisher of life. You knew me before I was born, and You formed every molecule of my genetic code. I ask You to heal me or guide me to the best solution. I hold on to Your promise that says You work all things together for good. I receive Your healing, Your guidance, and Your plan for my body in Christ's name, amen.

5. Discovering God's Direction for Your Family

How many people wish they had God's discernment to know who they should marry well before they say "I do"? How many parents feel the fear of not knowing what tomorrow will bring, and as a result lose sleep over how the future will impact their families?

We lived ten minutes from the girls' school. The teachers

were nice, and the facilities were new. It seemed like an ideal situation. Most of the teachers came from a religious affiliation similar to our own. There was only one problem: Many of the children who attended the school did not display such good character. They were verbally abusive to those who came from other countries. They used foul language and were disrespectful to their teachers. Our girls were miserable, and their grades were suffering.

There was another English-speaking school, but it definitely had its drawbacks. It was almost forty-five minutes from our house. It cost more money. And besides, I wasn't excited about our three little girls having a ninety-minute daily commute.

Since my wife is a missionary kid (someone who was raised on the mission field), I said, "Honey, we'll do whatever you feel is best for our girls." She prayed and asked the Lord for direction. Afterward, she felt a peace about changing schools, although at first I was reluctant. The first day after the change, the girls got off the bus and said, "We love it!"

The students were mild-mannered and displayed a wonderful culture of kindness to one another. The atmosphere was uplifting and conducive to a healthy learning environment. The one issue that concerned me, though, was the amount of time our girls would be on a school bus. Shortly thereafter, God opened a door for us to rent a nicer home within ten minutes of the school.

My wife prayed for God's direction for our family, and the Lord answered her prayer. In spite of my reluctance, His answer came, and His provision was clear.

How important is a decision like changing schools? What kind of impact does it have on a family or on children? I can tell you that it's not insignificant. It's huge. Pray for God's direction. It could be the most important thing you can do for your family.

If your family is not heading in the right direction, you can ask God for guidance. If you long to see your family moving forward and you desire to lead it out of survival mode to a place where it can thrive, then begin to ask Him to guide you, and He will.

A biblical prayer for guidance regarding family:

> Lord, my family needs Your help. We need Your direction and guidance. I ask You to help me pass on Your blessings to the generations that follow. Help us to serve You and become a family that walks in Your provision and protection. Help us to lay aside our pride and eliminate competition so that we can experience Your healing. Break the chains of generational dysfunction and set us free. I ask this in your precious name, amen.

III. Finding God's Direction When You Are Uncertain

There are times when the uncertainties that we face create instability in our hearts. When we feel unsure about the direction we should take, God is patient, and He will help us sort things out. No one understood that like Gideon.

The Israelites did evil in the eyes of the Lord. For seven years, their enemies crushed them. Every time there was a harvest, they invaded the entire territory and took everything. Not one living thing was spared from their wrath. The Israelites lived under such oppression that they were forced to find shelter in mountain clefts, caves, and strongholds. Finally, when things got unbearable, they cried out to the Lord for help.

Gideon was threshing the wheat in a winepress and hiding it from the Midianites. The angel of the Lord appeared to him and said, "The LORD is with you, mighty warrior." Gideon was a bit taken aback by the introduction. He wondered how God could be with them if so many awful things were happening in his country. "Our fathers told us of God's power," he said. "We were taught about the miracles that He performed when He rescued us from Egypt. But now it looks like the Lord has turned us over to Midian." Gideon was obviously blind to the fact that the Israelites caused their own demise because they did many evil things in the Lord's eyes.

Then the Lord responded, "Go with the strength you have, and rescue Israel from the Midianites. I am sending you!" Gideon replied, "But God, how can I save Israel? My clan is the weakest in the region, and I am the least in my family." "I am with you. You will eliminate the Midianites from your lands," the Lord responded. Then Gideon asked the question that everyone would want answered: "How do I know that it's really You talking with me? Give me a sign."

After preparing a sacrifice for Him, Gideon took some meat and unleavened bread and placed them on a rock and poured broth over them. The angel of the Lord reached out with His staff and touched the meat and bread. Suddenly, a fire flared from the rock and consumed it. Gideon was shocked. He realized at that moment that he wasn't just talking with an angel. He was talking with the one true God.

Soon all the enemies of Israel joined forces and gathered in the Valley of Jezreel. That's when the Spirit of the Lord came upon Gideon. He sent word throughout Manasseh calling all his allies to join him in battle. Then he inquired of the Lord once again: "If You will save Israel by my hand as You have promised—look, I will place a wool fleece on the threshing floor. If there is dew only on the fleece and all the ground is dry, then I will know that You will save Israel by my hand, as You said."

The next morning when Gideon got up to see what had taken place, he picked up the fleece. It was full of dew to the point that he wrung out a bowlful of water. Then Gideon asked for a second sign. This time, he reversed his request. Instead of the fleece having water in it with everything else dry, he asked the Lord to saturate the ground and leave the fleece completely dry. In order to show Gideon that He was with him, God did what Gideon asked.

Gideon was ready for battle. He had thirty-two thousand men ready to fight, but the Lord said, "You have too many men. You must dismiss all but three hundred of the best fighters." So after sending twenty-two thousand back home, he followed the Lord's direction. Gideon led them down to the water and separated those who drank the water by lifting it to their mouths in their hands from those who simply bent down like dogs and drank on their hands and knees. The Lord told him, "Keep the three hundred who drank the water from their hands."

The Lord then reassured him, saying, "I am going to give the Midianites into your hands." Still, Gideon was uncertain and understandably so. The Midianites, the Amalekites and many other people groups had converged together, and their numbers were too great to count. That's when the Lord told him to go into the Midian camp and listen to what the people were saying among themselves. Just as he arrived, a man was telling a friend about a dream. He said, "A round loaf of barley bread came tumbling into the Midianite camp. It struck the tent with such force that the tent overturned and collapsed." His friend responded, "This can be nothing other than the sword of Gideon son of Joash, the Israelite. God has given the Midianites and the whole camp into his hands."

When Gideon heard the dream, he was convinced that the Lord was guiding him every step of the way. All doubt was gone. His direction was crystal clear. That night the battle began, and he led three hundred warriors with a vengeance against the people groups that had oppressed Israel for seven long years. The Lord caused such great confusion in the Midian camp that their warriors turned on one another. Gideon pushed them out of the region and eliminated their leadership. His victory was uncontested, and every town that refused to give his soldiers food and water eventually paid a high price for their dissent. (Story paraphrased from Judges 6–8 NIV.)

God helped Gideon sort things out when he was unsure. He confirmed time and time again that He was with him and that He would guide him through the storm. Friend, I believe that God will do the same for you. He will not only help you see when things become cloudy, but He will also offer you His guidance during your darkest hour (Isa. 50:10).

Finding God's Direction During Your Time of Need or in the Midst of Crisis

"I'm sorry, sir. We cannot issue an APB on your daughter for at least twenty-four hours." Those words were the most haunting I've ever heard as a parent. At the time, we were living in San José, Costa Rica. Just one hour before that phone call, I sat down to work on my computer when my middle daughter, Chanel, asked if she could go outside and play. I asked her, "Where is Celina?"—her older sister. "I think she's at Priscilla's house," she replied. I said, "Sweetie, you can go outside, but only if your sister is with you." At the time, Celina was eight, and Chanel was six.

Five minutes later, my wife came in and kissed me good-bye. She took our one and only car to have lunch with a friend. Within minutes, I was back into the details of e-mail correspondence. After about thirty minutes, I got up and walked down the hallway and noticed that the girls were nowhere in sight. I called their names, but no one answered. After checking the backyard, I walked out front and saw Chanel sitting on the curb. I said, "Chanel, where is Celina?" She said, "I thought she was at Priscilla's house, but they said she left."

Without hesitating, I walked across the street to ask our neighbors if our daughter was there. The mom answered the door. I said, "Hello, is Celina here?" "No," she replied. "She left about an hour ago." All of a sudden, the world came to a grinding halt. "Why?" she asked. "Is there a problem?" I didn't even bother to answer her question. I sprinted back to our house and looked under every bed, in every closet, in the backyard, and in every favorite hiding place. Celina was nowhere to be found.

I made Chanel stay home in case Celina wandered back. In the meantime, I ran down to the corner store to see if she had gone to buy some candy. The owner said that he hadn't seen her all day. My concern turned to fear. I ran around the block yelling her name at the top of my lungs. People were coming out of their houses to see what was the matter. Still, no one had any information. No one saw a thing. My daughter was very responsible. She would never wander off. I feared the worst.

The fear that my eight-year-old little girl had been abducted began to overwhelm me. I remember vividly that finally, as I stood in the middle of our street with tears of fear and panic streaming down my face, I raised my voice to the Lord and said, "Please, God, direct me at this crucial time! Guide my actions and steps!"

Down deep inside I knew I needed to get ahold of my wife, but she had the car, and we had no cell phone. Although she probably mentioned which restaurant she was going to, for the life of me, I couldn't remember what she said. Unfortunately, I was confined to the house. I walked into my home office and picked up the phone to call the Costa Rican authorities. I located the police station just a mile from where we lived. I said, "Excuse me, sir, but I am a bit shaken by what has happened. I believe that my daughter has been abducted. Can you put out an All Points Bulletin?" "What was she wearing?" he asked. He might as well have asked me what the distance was from the moon to Neptune. I humiliatingly replied, "I can't remember." He said, "Do you remember what she looks like?" I said, "Yes, of course. She has blond hair and blue eyes." He said, "Well in Costa Rica, she will be easy to find. How many days has she been missing?" I said, "She's been missing for about an hour."

"An hour?" he said. "I'm sorry, sir. We cannot issue an APB on your daughter for at least twenty-four hours." My heart sank. I needed help, and I needed it fast. My daughter's life depended on it.

I asked God again to please guide me and help me during our time of need. Once again I felt that I needed to contact my wife. But how? I thought, *My wife loves the mall. She's probably there*. I called the mall and asked them to make a public announcement, but they said the PA system was out of service. I then called my favorite restaurant where they know all of us. My wife wasn't there. When I finally calmed down enough to remember her favorite restaurant, whose name I couldn't pronounce much less spell correctly, I called another missionary to find out the name of the place. After dialing 411 to get the number of Ponte Vecchio, the very popular Italian eatery, I made the call.

When the manager answered, I said, "Could you look through the restaurant to see if there are two redheads there? Specifically, I am looking for my wife. Her name is Cindee. If she is there, can you call her to the phone?" "Right away, sir." After what seemed to be an eternity, I heard a very familiar voice on the other end of the phone.

"Cindee?" I asked.

"Yes, Jason, what's up?"

"I have some very bad news, I'm afraid."

"What happened?" she replied.

"I don't even know how to tell you this, but it seems as though Celina has been abducted."

"What? What do you mean abducted? How did this happen?"

"Well, she was at Priscilla's house, and she left and never came home. She's gone."

"That's impossible," she said.

"I know it is," I replied.

"No, I mean she's not gone."

"What do you mean?" I asked.

"I told you before I left that I was driving her over to Stephanie's house. She's there right now."

Once again, the world stopped.

I wish that every story regarding a crisis could end like this one. I realize that many people suffer unbearable pain in the midst of tragedy. Some people might argue that I didn't need any direction because my daughter was never in danger. That's true. But I was, and that's the point of this story. In the middle of a ninety-minute highly turbulent storm, I needed guidance. From my perspective, life was out of control. I was convinced that my daughter had been abducted. In the middle of all the emotional chaos, the Lord tried to get a message to me twice. Eventually, I listened, and He led me back to a place of solid ground.

Do you feel like life is a bit out of control? Are you searching for solid ground? What prayer do you need answered? Where do you need direction? In what area do you seek God's leadership? Regardless of what you're facing, you can rest assured that God will guide you! What gives me the authority to make that statement? How can I say that God always answers the prayer of guidance? Because He always wants to lead! He always wants to guide. And, most important, He always wants us to follow. So when you pray for God's guidance, expect an answer, because it will come! *He is your guide.*

As we conclude this chapter, let me sum up what we've covered. If you are sincere and genuinely want God's guidance, He will show Himself faithful in every area of life.

Now let's focus our attention on the second prayer that God always answers, the prayer of forgiveness. It promises to give hope to the hopeless.

The prayers for direction included in this chapter can be summed up with this simple two-sentence prayer: *Lord, direct me. I give You total freedom to guide my steps.*

CHAPTER TWO

The Prayer for Forgiveness

The deputy carefully searched our belongings then motioned for us to walk through the metal detector. After the guard behind the one-inch-thick bulletproof glass pushed the button, the three-hundred-pound security door slammed behind us, echoing throughout the facility that held nearly a thousand inmates. "Clear!" the guard yelled. It was obvious that we had passed from a world of freedom into one that we had never seen before. To our left and right, prisoners silently stared at us as we made our way through the maze of the county jail.

My dear friend Pablo Kot, who serves as a chaplain in several of the jails in Southern California, invited me to speak to the general population and hand out paperback copies of my first book, *Power to Reinvent Yourself*. When I accepted the invitation, I had no idea what to expect.

I asked two friends to accompany me, Mel Van Meter and Dave Wilson. After we entered the concrete common area surrounded by twenty-foot security fences, we set up the portable sound system and prayed. At 8:30 a.m., the deputy walked over and announced that the first group was arriving. To say that I was nervous would be an understatement.

The prisoners nonchalantly strolled into the courtyard wearing orange jumpsuits with the acronym of the name of the detention center stenciled on their backs. Many were doing time because of drugs, others because of gang violence, others because of murder. The leaders found their preferential seating in the shade, while the newer inmates sat in the sun on the hot concrete. A few of them were sizable with an overall appearance of what you might expect for someone incarcerated. Some had long hair while others had crew cuts. Their ages ranged from eighteen to sixty-five. There were whites, African Americans, Hispanics, and Asians. Although I was taller than all of them, in my mind, I was convinced any one of them could whup me without any effort. Since this first group was made up entirely of ladies, you can imagine how I felt when I spoke to the men later that day.

I shared for twenty-five minutes and told my testimony about how the Lord rescued me from a crazy past filled with confusion and dysfunction. I concluded my message by saying, "God loves you and wants to forgive you. He sees you as the apple of His eye. If you want God's forgiveness today, please raise your hand so I can pray for you." Tears began to trickle down the cheeks of several of the ladies. Eighty-one women out of ninety raised their hands that morning.

After a short break, we headed to the yard to speak to the men. It was an acre of grass with a basketball court on cement. Most of the crusades we hold are in stadiums, sports arenas, or convention centers. We've never had armed guards posted in strategic locations. However, that afternoon was different. Deputies stood in towers with loaded rifles overlooking the courtyard. The men were escorted into the area single file. Their hands were folded together just above their waists. This time, a tall chain-link fence separated me from the inmates.

Just before I was introduced to speak, I glanced across a sea of orange uniforms. I noticed one young man in particular. He had a physical appearance like no other. His nickname was *Tarzan*. I've never seen a human being so buff, so cut, so muscular. He dropped to the ground and began to do push-ups but never stopped staring at me. It was intimidating to say the least. He was like a lion watching for the opportune moment to attack its prey.

After a twenty-five-minute message that concluded with my testimony, I asked the following question: "How many of you want God's forgiveness?" More than half raised their hands. Tarzan stopped his rigorous exercise regimen and stood to his feet. He continued to glare at me through the chain-link fence. After three seconds, which seemed like an eternity, his hand shot up in the air. That afternoon several hundred prisoners asked Christ to forgive them of their sins so they could begin a new life with God.

As I led the prisoners of the detention center in a simple prayer that day asking God to erase their spiritual debts, I realized that at the core of the human heart exists a vital need that only God can satisfy. While there are a few people who may seem indifferent, most want to be at peace with God. They want a sense that their outstanding debts are settled. Asking God to forgive us is the only way to fulfill that need. It's the only way we can make things right between God and us.

Perhaps you are carrying a huge weight on your shoulders and you feel emotionally and spiritually exhausted. You may even feel unclean because you've done things you're not proud of. If that is the case, this chapter aims to break down the walls that keep you from experiencing God's love and peace. This chapter will provide sound biblical principles along with real-world testimonies to demonstrate that God lifts the heavy burden of guilt for anyone (regardless of what he or she has done) who genuinely seeks His forgiveness.

First, we will look at different biblical examples of people who asked God to forgive them. Second, we will see how God's forgiveness can profoundly impact five specific areas of your life. The third section offers hope when you find it difficult to sense God's presence or feel His forgiveness. This chapter will serve as a powerful spiritual breakthrough in your life. As we begin, let's establish a biblical foundation in regard to the second prayer that God always answers: *the prayer for forgiveness.*

I. Biblical Examples of God Answering the Prayer for Forgiveness

The Bible refers to God's forgiveness for those who seek it more than twenty-five times in both the Old and the New Testaments. I've listed a few verses to help you see the way God responds to those who seek His forgiveness and the liberty that comes as a result of a repentant heart:

"O Lord, if I have found favor in your eyes," he said, "then let the Lord go with us. Although this is a stiff-necked people, forgive our wickedness and our sin, and take us as your inheritance." (Exodus 34:9)

In accordance with your great love, forgive the sin of these people, just as you have pardoned them from the time they left Egypt until now. (Numbers 14:19)

If my people, who are called by my name, will humble themselves and pray and seek my face and turn from their wicked ways, then will I hear from heaven and will forgive their sin and will heal their land. (2 Chronicles 7:14)

I acknowledged my sin to you and did not cover up my iniquity. I said, "I will confess my transgressions to the LORD"—and you forgave the guilt of my sin. (Psalm 32:5)

I will cleanse them from all the sin they have committed against me and will forgive all their sins of rebellion against me. (Jeremiah 33:8)

Forgive us our sins, for we also forgive everyone who sins against us. And lead us not into temptation. (Luke 11:4)

If we confess our sins, he is faithful and just and will forgive us our sins and purify us from all unrighteousness. (1 John 1:9)

These verses give us a clear biblical picture that God indeed forgives those who genuinely and sincerely seek His forgiveness. On the other hand, there are three specific times when He refused to forgive. In the instances below, there is a stern warning for those who have no remorse, who do not have a repentant heart. Not only is forgiveness out of the question, but also, those who practice wickedness will not inherit eternal life. Specifically, in the case of Manasseh, the impact of his unrepentant heart was felt for hundreds of years.

> Make sure there is no man or woman, clan or tribe among you today whose heart turns away from the LORD our God to go and worship the gods of those nations; make sure there is no root among you that produces such bitter poison. When such a person hears the words of this oath, he invokes a blessing on himself and therefore thinks, "I will be safe, even though I persist in going my own way." This will bring disaster on the watered land as well as the dry. The LORD will never be willing to forgive him; his wrath and zeal will burn against that man. All the curses written in this book will fall upon him, and the LORD will blot out his name from under heaven. (Deuteronomy 29:18–20)

> Joshua said to the people, "You are not able to serve the LORD. He is a holy God; he is a jealous God. He will not forgive your rebellion and your sins." (Joshua 24:19)

> Surely these things happened to Judah according to the LORD's command, in order to remove them from his presence because of the sins of Manasseh and all he

had done, including the shedding of innocent blood. For he had filled Jerusalem with innocent blood, and the LORD was not willing to forgive. (2 Kings 24:3–4)

It's worth noting that in these three passages, God doesn't lack the desire to forgive. But rather, people expressed no contrition. They showed no remorse for their mistakes and didn't repent. When people refuse to turn away from their self-centered sinful ways, God withholds His forgiveness (1 Cor. 6:9; Gal. 5:21).

In many ways, the instances mentioned above are similar to the unpardonable sin, blasphemy against the Holy Spirit (Matt. 12:31; Mark 3:29). Most Christian and Catholic scholars agree that this sin is the most serious of all spiritual transgressions. And while God offers no redemption for such an offense, there is no biblical account of someone sinning against the Lord in this way. Blasphemy implies a total irreverence and a complete rejection of God and His authority, and it would seem unlikely that the person who commits the unpardonable sin would seek His forgiveness.

So then, what must we possess in order for God to answer our prayer of forgiveness? Do we have to be perfect before we ask God to forgive us? Absolutely not! If that were the case, no one would qualify (Rom. 3:23). The only prerequisite is a genuine and sincere heart.

When you sincerely desire to be at peace with God, and you are willing to be transparent about your shortcomings, God will stretch out His loving arms and embrace you. Much like the prodigal son who returned to his father expecting a strong rebuke, you will hear the words "My child was once lost and now is found." He will empower you to turn from the things that have held you in spiritual captivity. As long as your heart is genuine, you can rest assured that you will receive His pardon. I have yet to discover anywhere in the Bible where God refused to forgive a person who sincerely sought His forgiveness.

Over the years, I have talked with tens of thousands of people. Their stories are similar in many ways. Many feel they carry a burden, a heavy weight on their shoulders. But when they come to the point of asking God to forgive them, they say it is as if a huge load suddenly lifts. There is a sense of spiritual cleansing that comes over them.

Do you feel like you are carrying an overwhelming burden? Have you become entangled in things that have produced destructive and sinful patterns in your life? When you look in the mirror, do you feel clean? Do you like what you see? Or do you have spiritual debts? If you want to experience freedom from the heavy burden of guilt, consider the following prayer. I have pieced together what some of the great people of the Bible have said when they sought God's forgiveness. In every case, God responded positively. If you pray this prayer with sincerity, I have no doubt that He will forgive you.

The Prayer for Forgiveness

Lord, I have fallen short in many ways, and I know what I have done is wrong. I don't offer You any excuses. Instead, I offer You a heart that seeks Your acceptance and love. I believe You are a loving God. So I ask You to forgive me, Lord, for sinning against You and anyone else I have affected. Now please give me the power to change so I can walk in Your freedom. In Christ's name I pray, amen.

This prayer for forgiveness covers many areas where people feel they fail spiritually and ethically. The prayer is general and is meant to help people become reconciled in their relationship with God. I carry a conviction, however, that praying with specificity is always better, because it allows us to grow and see progress in the areas where sin has kept us in bondage.

I have outlined five different areas where you can apply the prayer for forgiveness in order to experience a powerful spiritual breakthrough in the struggles you face. Why is this so important? Because when we continue to carry a heavy burden and do not wipe the slate clean, we cannot think clearly. When we lack the strength to resist temptation, we are more likely to fall into the same traps again and again.

However, when we ask God to forgive us and the heavy burden we have carried suddenly lifts, we gain more strength to walk away from the temptations that lured us in the first place. Forgiveness allows us to start a new chapter, and it gives us strength to combat temptation. If you have struggled with sexual promiscuity, poor parenting or disrespecting your parents, immoral behavior, materialism, or turning away from the Lord, the following five areas will empower you to overcome the traps that keep you bound.

It's worth noting that several of the areas mentioned in this chapter deal with our relationships with other people. While it may—or may not—be appropriate for you to go to those you have hurt, abused, or have had inappropriate relationships with and ask for forgiveness, this book concentrates on prayer, not interpersonal relationships. The following five areas are meant to help you set the record straight between you and God.

II. How the Prayer for Forgiveness Can Empower You in Five Areas Where People Fail the Most

1. Experiencing Forgiveness for Sexual Promiscuity— The Seventh Commandment (Exodus 20:14)

Close to 45 percent of all high school students lose their virginity by the time they graduate.[1] While it's true that some people don't care about the implications of their sexual activities, a large percentage feel a strong conviction about right and wrong, and they feel that in spite of their mistakes, sexual intimacy should be kept between a husband and a wife.

Feelings of guilt for premarital sex, adultery, and fornication can linger for years. But God welcomes everyone who has fallen short with open arms. If you are truly sorry for what has taken place, God will forgive you.

King David was a man after God's own heart. He worshipped the Lord like no other world leader. God gave him everything he needed and much more. God would have given him even more if he had asked (2 Sam. 12:8). Unfortunately, David had a problem. The beauty of his neighbor's wife overwhelmed his sense of good judgment.

A man named Uriah was married to Bathsheba. One night while he was off at war, Bathsheba was bathing in her backyard. David was walking on the roof of his palace and saw her from a distance. So he sent for her.

Their adulterous affair was quick, and within weeks, she sent word to him saying she was pregnant. David tried to cover his immorality by devising a plan to bring Uriah home from the war and give him an opportunity to sleep with his wife. That way, Uriah would think that the child was his. To David's dismay, Uriah refused, because his fellow countrymen were still fighting on the front lines.

In a moment of desperation, David arranged to have Uriah killed, and he took Bathsheba to be his wife. For weeks he thought his secret was safe, until, finally, the Lord sent the prophet Nathan to confront him. Nathan walked into the palace and said, "Why did you despise the word of the LORD by doing what is evil in his eyes? You struck down Uriah the Hittite with the sword and took his wife to be your own" (2 Sam. 12:9).

David's reply was contrite and heartfelt: "I have sinned against the LORD," he said (12:13). Then Nathan replied, "The LORD has taken away your sin. You are not going to die. But... the son born to you will die" (v. 13). Indeed, that would be the case. David repented, and God forgave him. David was in good standing once again. After the death of his son, Bathsheba bore David a second son. His name was Solomon.

While it might seem painful and dreadful to humble ourselves and ask God to forgive our spiritual iniquities, He hears our prayers and helps us begin the process of putting our lives back together again.

Just remember, the God of the universe forgave David for despicable acts. If God would be willing to extend His arms of forgiveness to a voyeur, an adulterer, and a murderer, why wouldn't He do the same for you?

If you have failed, God wants you to know that you can begin a new chapter. You can experience freedom from the burden of guilt. He extends His loving arms of forgiveness for whatever sexual transgression you have committed. Today can be the beginning of a new chapter for you.

Here is a prayer I have outlined that will be helpful for

you. If your past has been tainted with premarital sex, adultery, or fornication, the Lord will respond positively to your request for forgiveness, and the only thing He requires of you is a sincere heart.

> Lord, I have sinned against You and someone who is precious to You. I had poor judgment, and as a result, brought shame and embarrassment upon others and myself. I don't offer You an excuse. I won't try to justify my actions. Instead, I ask You to forgive me and lift the burden of guilt that I carry. Please make me whole again and restore me as a child of God who is in good standing with You. I ask You to renew my mind and empower me to face future temptation. In Christ's name I pray, amen.

2. Experiencing Forgiveness for Poor Parenting or Disrespecting Our Parents—The Fifth Commandment (Exodus 20:12; Colossians 3:21, Ephesians 5:22–6:4)

Sinning Against Our Children

Have you ever made a significant mistake as a parent? Has your child pushed you beyond your limits of patience, and, as a result, you have been unduly harsh with him or her? Perhaps you lost your temper and became abusive. When parents overreact, sooner or later they feel guilty. God uses that guilt as a sign to help them steer away from their emotionally and physically destructive behavior.

On the other hand, you might not be short-tempered or abusive at all. Maybe you are just the opposite. Could it be that you hardly spend time with your children or that you neglect them emotionally? Do you find it difficult to listen to them, play with them, or be supportive in a way you know they deserve? In the same way guilt serves to steer us from overreacting, it also 'works to draw us closer to our children.

If you feel guilty for the poor choices you have made as a parent, your first step is to make things right with God.

Some might argue, "Parents shouldn't be seeking God's forgiveness. They should be seeking the forgiveness of their children." Although I believe that parents should seek their children's forgiveness in most instances, it's not true in every case. There are times when clearing our own consciences appeases only us. Instead of helping others, it brings up wounds from the past and causes even greater pain in the hearts of those from whom we seek forgiveness. In every case when we sin, however, we must seek God's pardon. If we don't, the consequences are severe and will impact the generations that follow. The story of Samuel and Eli exemplifies this point very well.

Samuel lay down next to the lamp. Just before he fell asleep, he heard someone call his name. He sprang up and ran to the older man in the next room. "Here I am. What do you want?" "I did not call; go back and lie down, Samuel," Eli said. So he went and lay down. Within minutes, he heard his name again. Running back to Eli for a second time, the old man responded, "I didn't call you. Now go back to bed." Still, Samuel heard the voice again. This time when Samuel went into Eli's room, the old man discerned that it was the Lord who was speaking to the young boy. He told him, "Go and lie down, and if He speaks to you again, say, 'Speak, Lord, for Your servant is listening.'" So Samuel did as he was told.

Within minutes the Lord spoke to Samuel again, and the boy replied, "Speak, Lord. Your servant is listening." The Lord said, "See, I am about to do something in Israel that will make the ears of everyone who hears of it tingle. At that time I will carry out against Eli everything I spoke against his family—from beginning to end. For I told him that I would judge his family forever because of the sin he knew about; his sons made themselves contemptible, and he failed to restrain them. Therefore, I swore to the house of Eli, 'The guilt of Eli's house will never be atoned for by sacrifice or offering.'"

The next morning Eli asked Samuel if the Lord spoke to him, and Samuel said, "Yes, He did." "What did He say to you?" The boy was somewhat reluctant to respond to his mentor. Eli became adamant, saying, "May God deal with you ever so severely unless you tell me every detail of your conversation." To that the young boy replied, "Very well, master. The Lord says, 'For the evil things you allowed your sons to do, you and your family will not be forgiven.'" Eli's response was indifferent: "He is the LORD; let him do what is good in his eyes."

Eli was the high priest, the holiest man in the land. Because he allowed his sons to do detestable things, including sleeping with all the women who worked at the entrance of the Tent of Meeting, God's anger burned against him. He failed terribly as a parent and neglected to raise his sons in the ways of the Lord. As a result of his sinful neglect, the generations that followed him paid a high price.

If Eli had asked God to forgive him and taken steps to correct his negligent behavior, God's judgment could have been averted. Instead, he was uninterested in making the right choices as a parent and showed contempt as a follower of God's laws. (Story paraphrased from 1 Samuel 3 NIV.) As the story of Eli illustrates, parents can be very negligent. The following story demonstrates how abusive they can become over something of little significance.

At 2:00 a.m., the six children woke up to a fierce argument. Their father had come home drunk for the fifth time that week, and their mother tried to keep him quiet. His violent temper and overwhelming size were too much for any member of the family. He stormed into the garage, pulled out a baseball bat, and raised it above his head. "Everyone out!" he exclaimed. His wife corralled the children, grabbed a large blanket, and herded them out the front door.

The children and their mother sat on the curb in the pouring rain until the next morning. When the family returned to the house at 8:00 a.m., the father woke up without a clue as to what had happened the night before. The nightmare was not uncommon for the family.

The next day the oldest brother, who lived with his wife and children, found out what happened. He confronted his father: "If you don't stop your destructive behavior, you will lose your wife, children, and everything else you hold dear to your heart. Do you love your sin more than you love your family?" The father broke down and wept. "I have nowhere to turn. I have no one to help me. What can I do?" The son replied, "Come with me to a meeting where you can find help." That week, he walked into his first Alcoholics Anonymous meeting.

After asking God to forgive him, he went to his wife and children and did the same. God was gracious to him. Nearly fifteen years have passed, and today, his relationship with God and his family have never been better.

Some might say, "Yes, my husband can be abusive, but I am not." In the homes where the husband is abusive and the wife remains silent (or vice versa), she is committing the same horrific act of violence. How? Instead of protecting the lives of her children, her silence protects his sinful behavior. She has chosen to align herself with someone who is doing evil.

Or others might say, "I don't mistreat my kids, and I don't allow them to do detestable things." My question to those parents is, "But do you spend the time with your children that you should? Do you listen to them? Do you nurture them and raise them as a parent should? Or have you been negligent in some way?" Parental neglect is one of the main reasons young people fall into delinquency.[2]

If you are a parent who has made grave mistakes and carries a load of guilt, God extends to you His loving arms of forgiveness, provided that you are genuinely sorry for the choices you have made. When your heart is sincere, God provides a way to move beyond your sinful behavior. If you desire to set the record straight with God, the following prayer will guide you to a place of forgiveness in your role as a parent:

Lord, I feel I have not measured up as a parent. You entrusted the precious lives of my children to me, and at times I haven't displayed the best judgment in raising them. Forgive me, Lord. Help me to be a better parent. Help me to transmit Your love, Your affection, Your patience, Your strength, Your steadfastness, and Your integrity to them. Help me to wipe the slate clean and begin again. I want to be a great example and have the credibility to restore my relationship with my children. In Christ's name, amen.

Sinning Against Our Parents

Watching your children leave home can be one of the most difficult challenges in life. The other is watching your parents grow old. In the same way that we should strive to be excellent parents, it is important that we honor our parents. Honor doesn't mean that we say yes to every request. It doesn't mean that we must be in constant agreement with them. It doesn't mean that we go against our better judgment and obey their orders. It simply means that the tone of our words and actions shows esteem for their position in our lives, the position that God gave them (Exod. 20:12).

Most of the time I am a decent son, but down deep inside I know that I have failed many times. There were moments when my tone did not reflect the respect that my parents deserved. Like many children, I displayed an arrogant, self-important attitude that disregarded their wishes and input. Sadly, children don't outgrow those attitudes when they become adults.

Absalom was the most attractive man in Israel (2 Sam. 14:25). As the son of King David, he could have had anything he wanted. The one thing he lacked, unfortunately, was respect for his father. I'm quite certain that some scholars would argue that David was neglectful. Still, when Absalom had children of his own, he became obsessed with killing his father and ascending to the throne. Absalom's life ended in tragedy in the midst of a battle. When he became caught in the branches of an oak tree, David's soldiers gathered around and slaughtered him. Although David's life was spared, he was devastated. Whenever children lose respect for their parents and hold them in contempt, nothing good ever results.

As a minister, I have had the honor of counseling thousands of people in the past twenty years. During the course of sharing their personal struggles with me, many divulge how they feel about their parents. It's sad to see how many people identify, in part, with the prodigal son. They wish they could say, *Just give me my inheritance and get out of my life!*

Forgiveness, respect, and honor are not emotions. They are shown through actions based upon choices. We decide to do them even when we don't feel like it. When we decide to respect and honor our parents, the door opens for God's forgiveness to enter our lives. Perhaps you have broken the fifth commandment and have not honored your parents. If you feel resentment toward them yet desire to release your bitter feelings, God wants you to experience freedom. The only way you can experience freedom is through forgiveness. And the only way you can experience forgiveness is by asking Him for it. If you sincerely ask God to pardon your mistakes, you can begin a new day in your relationships with God and your parents.

This prayer aims to help you ask God for forgiveness in regard to your relationship with your parents. I am confident that God will answer this simple prayer:

Lord, I have not honored my father and mother like I should. My pride has prevented me from seeing them the way You do. I do not want to harbor anger, bitterness, or resentment toward them. Forgive me for disrespecting them and help me to honor them in a way that is pleasing to You. Guide my steps and my heart in this process. I pray this in Christ's name, amen.

3. Experiencing Forgiveness for Unethical and Immoral Behavior—The Sixth, Eighth, and Ninth Commandments (Exodus 20:13, 15–16)

When I was a child, my family dropped into church once or twice a year. In spite of our infrequent attendance, my parents emphatically taught me that it was wrong to lie, cheat, steal, and commit murder. My grandmother reinforced that teaching on the weekends as well. It seems shocking that such behavior in some circles is permissible provided you don't get caught. How many celebrities are remorseful for their immoral behavior only after the story breaks in the news? How many politicians believe they are exempt from the law? How many people are honest when preparing their taxes? Today our society fails to maintain a decent moral standard, and people continue to commit horrible acts against strangers, their neighbors, their friends, and yes, even their families.

The father of the Judeo-Christian faith committed such an act. Abraham went to Egypt with his wife, Sarah, to avoid a devastating famine. When they arrived, Abraham said to his wife, "I know what a beautiful woman you are. When the Egyptians see you, they will say, 'This is his wife.' Then they will kill me but will let you live. Say you are my sister, so that I will be treated well for your sake and my life will be spared because of you" (Gen. 12:11–13).

When Pharaoh's officials saw her beauty, they escorted her to their king. Pharaoh treated Abraham very well because of Sarah and gave him sheep, cattle, donkeys, camels, menservants, and maidservants. While Abraham was enjoying the benefits of pretending to be Sarah's brother, something tragic happened. God struck Pharaoh's household with serious diseases because he had taken Sarah to be his wife.

The king called Abraham into his chambers. "What have you done to me?" he demanded. "You told me this woman was your sister, and now I discover that she is your wife! Here, take her and go!" (Gen. 12:18–19, author's paraphrase).

What seemed to be an innocent manipulation of the facts turned out to be something that could have destroyed a nation. Even the father of faith was capable of questionable conduct. After that embarrassing time for Abraham and his wife, he left that area and headed north. There God gave Abraham and Sarah a new start and greatly prospered their family (Gen. 13:2).

Everyone, including Abraham, needs forgiveness. Every person has an account to settle with God. Whether we lie, cheat, steal, or in Moses' case, take the life of another man, we all need God's forgiveness. No one is perfect. No one is inherently holy. We all carry the seeds of destruction (Rom. 3:23).

Perhaps you might say, "I don't lie, cheat, or steal, and I've haven't killed anyone." While that may be the case, you may harbor hatred in your heart toward others. Holding people in contempt isn't healthy. It's not godly. Just like lying, cheating, and stealing, it must be reconciled.

If you struggle with telling the truth, being honest, taking what doesn't belong to you, or harboring hatred in your heart, God offers you hope for change. He offers you reconciliation, a brand-new start. If you want to apply the prayer for forgiveness specifically to an area of your life where you have failed morally or ethically, consider the following prayer as an example:

> Lord, I am morally bankrupt and I know that I have failed You. I haven't been honest with You or myself. I thought I could fool everyone. Forgive me for being deceptive and for behaving in such an inappropriate manner. I want to be in good standing with You. I want to make peace with You. Please help me to live a life full of holiness and integrity. I ask Your forgiveness in Christ's name, amen.

4. Experiencing Forgiveness for Materialism—The Tenth Commandment (Exodus 20:17)

Recently, I got up at 2:45 a.m. and drove to the closest outdoor mall. Between my house and my destination, there were four other cars on the freeway. I drove into the parking lot and discovered there were ninety people who had formed an unofficial line leading up to the entrance.

By the time the doors opened, the line had swelled to well over twenty-five hundred people and stretched beyond four football-field lengths. Why? We all had one thing in common. We were in search of the newest, most technologically advanced smartphone available. Yes, I admit it. I stood in line for nine hours. When I finally reached the front counter, the salesperson looked at me with a manufactured smile and asked, "So, are you excited about getting your new phone?" I said, "Of course not. I've been standing in line since 3:00 a.m. I have to go to the bathroom. I'm hungry, exhausted, and irritable, and for what? A phone! To be honest, I am somewhat embarrassed. But," I continued with a smirk, "at least I am not alone."

Why did I make such an effort? Because *I had to have it*. Indeed, materialism comes as a result of coveting things.

It's amazing what people will do for a gadget, money, power, or an experience. Since the Industrial Revolution, history has taught us that humanity becomes more materialistic with each passing decade. People are becoming less important than things, and when that happens, families fall apart and human depravity reaches a new low.

Let me make an important distinction. There is a difference between acquiring wealth because of good stewardship and consuming things at the expense of our relationships with God, family, neighbors, and friends. I believe that God wants us to move forward and walk in His blessings but not at the expense of others. When places, experiences and things become more important to us than God, we find ourselves in deep trouble. Lot's family learned this the hard way.

Four times Lot argued with the angels of the Lord. Four times he conveyed his reluctance to leave Sodom and Gomorrah. In spite of the stern warning coming from God's messengers, Lot and his family had no desire to leave their precious life in the wicked city. When the angels finally convinced Lot to urge those who were close to him to flee, his future sons-in-law disregarded the warning as a joke.

Soon, there was a knock at the door. The wicked men of the city demanded that Lot turn over the two visitors so they could have sex with them. Lot pleaded but to no avail. In a swift move, the angels grabbed Lot by the back of the collar and pulled him back inside the house. Then they stretched out their hands and struck the evil men of that town with blindness so they couldn't find the door.

Still, Lot was hesitant. He didn't want to leave. That's when the angels took him and the hands of his wife and daughters and led them safely out of the city. They gave them three specific orders: "Flee for your lives! Don't look back, and don't stop anywhere in the plain!"

At daybreak, Lot and his family approached a small town called Zoar. When the sun rose over the land, the Lord rained down burning sulfur from heaven and devoured the cities of Sodom and Gomorrah.

Was it the material wealth, the sexual perversion, or the libertine lifestyle that caused the destruction of the cities? No one really knows. One thing is certain. Something burned in the heart of Lot's wife. The thought of living a single moment outside the city was too much for her to handle. As the couple reached Zoar, she turned and faced that which she coveted and instantly became a pillar of salt, petrified from head to toe. (Story paraphrased from Genesis 19 NIV.)

I am quite sure that if we could ask his wife why she looked back knowing everything the city represented, her answer would be simple. She would reply, *Because I had to.* People who covet lose their sense of self-discipline. Their passions burn out of control. When people ardently pursue the things they don't need or shouldn't have, they go further into debt, sacrifice important relationships, get fat, or wind up dead. Sodom and Gomorrah was the epitome of covetousness, and Lot's wife paid for her covetousness with her life.

Jesus understood the dangers of coveting. He summed up everything I want to say in Luke 12:15: "Watch out! Be on your guard against all kinds of greed; a man's life does not consist in the abundance of his possessions."

Friend, are you frustrated because you are not where you want to be? Is the grass always greener on the other side of the fence? If you struggle with coveting things in a materialistic world, God opens a door of redemption for you. Even if you turned back and sinfully embraced something you shouldn't have or that didn't belong to you, God offers you the hand of forgiveness. If you regret your mistakes, ask Him to help you settle your account.

When I find myself walking down the path of covetousness, there is one person who is always willing to forgive and grant me the strength to change course. This is a biblical prayer that I know will help you at this time:

> Lord, sometimes the desires of my heart have led me off course. I have pursued things that I know were not beneficial for my relationships with You and others, all because I had to. Forgive me for coveting in my heart. I don't want to be driven by materialism. Instead, I want You to lead me. I ask You to renew my mind and give me a fresh start this day. In Christ's name I pray, amen.

5. Experiencing Forgiveness for Turning Your Back on God—The First, Second, Third, and Fourth Commandments (Exodus 20:1–11)

The first four areas of forgiveness that we discussed in this chapter deal with our interactions with other people. This area deals exclusively with our relationship with God. The first four commandments that the Lord gave us in Exodus 20 lay out the guidelines regarding our relationship with Him. If we violate these commandments, the repercussions will negatively impact the generations that follow us.

In essence, the first four commandments state that God should be the most important person in our lives. There should be nothing that comes between us. When we seek the pleasure that comes from addictions, idol worship, or other habitual behaviors that draw us away from Him, we become guilty of turning our backs on the Lord and breaking the first four commandments. Perhaps one of the classic biblical examples of someone who turned his back on God is found in Luke 15.

The young man got up one morning and walked in to see his father. "Dad, I think it's time that you divide your estate between my brother and me. Why don't you give me my inheritance now, so I can get on with my life?" The father was disappointed to hear his son's words. Nonetheless, the young man was old enough to make decisions on his own. So the father reluctantly granted his request.

Not too long after that, the son headed out the door with a new lease on life. With a large amount of wealth at his disposal, he went to a faraway country and began to spend his inheritance on whatever whim blew his way, sparing no expense. For a time, he found the perfect cure for boredom and forgot about his previous life.

Although his inheritance carried him for a while, it eventually ran out. With it went all the parties and fun adventures. Soon he had nothing. To make matters worse, a famine spread throughout the entire country, and there was no relief in sight. He had no choice but to get a job.

The only available work was feeding pigs. Fortunately, a local citizen paid him to carry pods used to feed the animals. He became hungry and yearned to grab a handful of the feed and fill his mouth in the same way the pigs ate every day.

Then something miraculous took place. Because no one would give him something to eat, he came to his senses. He said to himself, *How many of my father's workers have food to spare, and here I sit starving to death?! I will go back to my father and say to him: Father, I have sinned against heaven and against you. I am no longer worthy to be called your son; make me like one of your hired men.* That is, in fact, what he did. At this point, the only thing he owned was the clothes on his back. Not even his sandals were in good enough condition to carry him home.

The journey was long, which gave him sufficient time to rehearse his speech. As he entered the outskirts of the immense property, his father recognized his appearance from a great distance. Filled with compassion, he ran to his son, threw his arms around him, and kissed him. This was the moment he had prepared for during the entire trip. "Father," he said, "I have sinned against heaven and against you. I am no longer worthy to be called your son." Before he could say, "Make me like one of your hired men," his father interrupted him.

"Bring the best robe for my son," he said to one of his servants. "Put some sandals on his feet and a ring on his finger. Bring the fattened calf and kill it. Let's have a feast and celebrate. For this son of mine was dead and is alive again; he was lost and is found."

When the older brother discovered that his younger brother had returned, he wasn't pleased. In his mind, it wasn't fair that he had taken half the family's inheritance and squandered it on parties and prostitutes. Then he had the gall to return home with the hopes of living as he had before. The father pulled the older brother aside and said, "Son, you are my firstborn. Everything I have is yours. But your brother was lost. He was dead for all practical purposes. Today, however, we discovered that he is alive. He is your brother, and that alone is reason to celebrate."

The moment of redemption for the young man didn't come when his father saw him from a distance. It didn't come when he said, "Father, I have sinned against heaven and against you." It occurred when he *came to his senses* sitting in the midst of a herd of pigs. That's when he realized the error of his ways.

The above story, paraphrased from Luke 15:11–32 (NIV), portrays the heart of God toward those who turn their backs on Him. Whether people reject God's rules or embrace some sort of idol, the Lord looks at them with a heart of compassion. Although they have chosen to walk down a path of self-destruction, God wants to redeem and forgive them of all transgressions.

We can stop the pattern of destructive behavior. It doesn't have to pass from one generation to the next. How? The first step in breaking the pattern is realizing the error of our ways. Redemption begins when we come to our senses. If you want to reconcile your life with God and you sense that you have turned your back on Him, consider the following prayer as a guide to help you reconnect your life to Him:

Lord, help me come to my senses. I want to see my life as You do. Sometimes the excitement and euphoria that I so fervently pursue blinds my ability to think straight. I let things come between You and me, and as a result, I haven't spent the time with You that I should. I do not want any addictions or idols to come between us. Give me the strength, love, and power to make You the most important person in my life. In Christ's name I pray, amen.

III. Finding Hope When You Least Expect It

My parents were separated when I was three and divorced when I was nine. My mom remarried when I was fifteen. My family struggled with addiction and discord. Between my three parents, there are nine divorces. The first time I walked into a nondenominational church, I did not need to hear that I was a sinner. I felt like an outsider as soon as I got out of the car. I knew I had a spiritual problem, and I was ready to do something about it. I needed the power to break the sinful pattern over my life.

The family that invited me to church that Sunday night cheerfully escorted me through the lobby and down to the front of the church. Of all the places to sit as a first-time guest, the front row wasn't my preferred choice. Soon the music was under way, and the strangest thing happened. Several people raised their hands. I wasn't sure if they had a question or if they were trying to reach out to God. Soon I discovered that they were expressing their worship to the Creator of the universe.

The pastor began his message talking about the God who loves people and doesn't want to condemn. Again, several people responded in a way that was new for me. Almost on cue they would agree by verbalizing, "Amen!" and "That's right!" There was one statement the pastor shared that has stuck with me to this day. It resounded in my heart like nothing I had ever heard. He said, "Christ died for the sins of the world and has the power to transform any life." He then asked the question that changed my life: "Do you want to experience new life?"

Something happened that night. I didn't see any fireworks, and to be completely honest, I didn't feel much different than when I entered the building. I was certain of one thing, though. I heard what I needed to hear, and I was beginning the spiritual journey God wanted me to begin. I knew I was exactly where I needed to be. I found hope when I least expected it.

Unlike my experience, there are some people who feel they are *good*, and because of that, they hold the belief that God will cut them some sort of break. There is only one problem with that belief, however. Being *good* isn't good enough (Eph. 2:8–9).

Regardless of our family backgrounds or the way we feel about ourselves, each of us carries the potential for breaking God's laws. We all have a sinful nature, and our spiritual debts must be reconciled. The good news is that when we open our mouths and pronounce the words "God, I am sorry. Please forgive my sin," we've taken a huge step in our spiritual development.

True spiritual freedom can come when we open our hearts, confess to the Lord our sins, and ask Him to forgive us. This is where transformation takes place in the lives of those who come to Christ. When we live transparent lives before the Lord and sincerely ask Him to forgive us, strongholds are broken, chains are shattered, and prison doors begin to open. People who have been held captive for years suddenly see the light as the power of God sets them free.

How can I make the statement that God always responds to the prayer for forgiveness? Because He sent His Son to atone for every sin ever committed! He felt that your soul was worth sending His Son to the cross so that your spiritual debts would be settled. "What I received I passed on to you as of first importance: that Christ died for our sins according to the Scriptures" (1 Cor. 15:3). At the moment Christ died on the cross, every sin became pardonable, provided that the offender is genuinely repentant. "Christ died for sins once for all, the righteous for the unrighteous, to bring you to God. He was put to death in the body but made alive by the Spirit" (1 Pet. 3:18). So when you ask God to forgive you, expect that He will! *He is your forgiver.*

As we look back over this chapter, I trust that you can see God's undying love for you in spite of the mistakes you have made. This chapter deals with God's redemption and forgiveness that cover many areas where we fall short. If you are guilty of sexual promiscuity, poor parenting, disrespecting others, immoral conduct, materialism, or turning your back on the Lord, I hope you can see how God is willing to forgive you for breaking His commandments. He truly wants to restore your relationship with Him. Why? Because He considers you the apple of His eye (Zech. 2:8).

Friend, if you find it difficult to sense God's presence and forgiveness, I know exactly how you feel. In the midst of our doubts and disappointments, either we can listen to our feelings or we can hold on to God's truth as revealed in the pages of this chapter. If God can bring redemption to my life, imagine what He can do in yours. Indeed, there is good news for you today. Take time to reflect on the prayer for forgiveness and remind yourself that God's forgiveness comes as a result of His steadfast love and not as a result of the way you feel. In the coming days and weeks, you will sense God's powerful love for you.

The prayers of forgiveness listed in this chapter can be summed up with this simple two-sentence prayer: *Lord, forgive me. Cleanse me of my transgressions and renew my life today.*

CHAPTER THREE

The Prayer for Freedom

M anuel was seventeen years old when he decided to make a better life for himself. He told his mother that he was moving to Mexico where he could make three times as much money as he made in his home country. He caught a flight out of Central America and landed in Mexico City, knowing all along that his final destination was New Jersey. After a twenty-two-hour trip to the border, he crossed into San Diego illegally and was apprehended in Chula Vista, California. The authorities put him on a prison bus headed to a youth detention center.

Jail was never part of his plan. He was scared. He felt alone. He had one phone call. So he called his uncle who lived in the San Diego area. The two had never previously met.

When Manuel walked into his cell, it wasn't at all what he expected. His room had carpeting, cable television, air-conditioning, and he shared a bathroom with only one other person. He was able to see a doctor whenever he wanted. A chaplain held church services once a week, and during the mealtimes, he could go back for seconds. *This is not bad at all*, he thought.

His uncle Pedro arrived at the jail with the necessary paperwork. The guard called Manuel to the window where he met the man who had come to post his bail. Pedro said, "I'm here to get you out. Your paperwork should be in order by the end of the day." Manuel replied, "No thanks!" "Excuse me?" Pedro asked. "Did you say, 'No thanks'?" "Yes. I have all the amenities here in my room. I have air-conditioning, cable television, wall-to-wall carpeting, a view of the airport, three meals a day, and access to a doctor twenty-four hours a day. I live better here than I did in my own country. I've decided that I'm staying." Pedro couldn't believe his ears. After fifteen minutes he finally gave up and said, "I'll be back tomorrow."

Given the fact that Manuel was a minor, he didn't have much leverage in the legal system. Pedro returned the next day and asked the guard to call the adolescent. Manuel sat down in front of the window and picked up the phone. Pedro said, "The freedom that awaits you outside these four walls is so much greater than the amenities you have here. Look at yourself, for crying out loud. You're in jail! Your ignorance led you out of Central America. Your illegal actions brought you to this place. Your stubbornness keeps you here. You better wise up and take advantage of the opportunity to experience freedom." Although Manuel was reluctant at first, he finally agreed and walked out of the detention center later that afternoon.

He moved to New Jersey, and occasionally sent word back to his mother that he was making money and living the American Dream. But that was far from the truth.

Within two years, he was being investigated for alleged delinquent activities and was forced to return to his home country.

After returning to Central America, a family member asked him to explain his actions over the past twenty-four months. "Do you see a pattern here?" she asked. "You've tried to run things on your own, but instead of improving your life, you keep repeating the same mistakes." He suddenly realized that although he lived as a free man, very little had changed from the two days he spent in the detention center. Drugs, drinking, and wild living all contributed to his life in bondage.

That night, he had a powerful *aha!* moment and decided to turn his life over to the One who liberates those who are oppressed. He recognized the error of his ways and turned to God for deliverance, and God answered his prayer.

Ten years later and after attending ministry school, Manuel and his wife traveled throughout Central America with our missionary team, sharing with others about God's power to set the captive free. Today he pastors a church of five hundred and frequently travels internationally without incident.

Manuel is an excellent example of someone who, with God's help, managed to break free from the vicious cycle that kept him bound. His story illustrates that God can transform anyone. He can break any cycle. You, my friend, are no exception to that truth. God can help you break free from the things that have held you back for years. God can give you the freedom you seek.

I've discovered that people are, in some ways, much like Manuel not wanting to leave his jail cell. They become attached to their prison. They love their vices, addictions,

THE SEVEN PRAYERS GOD ALWAYS ANSWERS

turmoil, conflict, and depressive existence. When invited to leave their emotional and spiritual incarceration behind, their initial reaction is, "No thanks! I like my four walls of confinement. My shackles fit me just fine. I've got everything I need." Not until they get a glimpse of the real freedom that only God offers are they able to realize that they bought a lie.

This chapter will help you tap into the power of God that liberates, delivers, and sets the captive free. As you lift up the prayers in this chapter, the chains in your life will begin to break. I have divided it into three sections. First, we will lay a biblical foundation for the prayer for freedom, looking at the different verses where people reached out to God and experienced His liberating power. The second section shows how to apply the prayer for freedom to the four areas where people struggle the most. Finally, the third section offers hope and will inspire you to get up and walk through the door to freedom that God offers you. Now let's turn our focus to establishing a biblical foundation to the third prayer that God always answers: *the prayer for freedom.*

I. Biblical Examples of God Answering the Prayer for Freedom

The Bible refers to the power of God that delivers those who ask Him more than twenty-five times in both the Old and the New Testaments. The following verses illustrate how God empowers us to live lives of freedom when we call on the name of the Lord:

O LORD our God, deliver us from his hand, so that all kingdoms on earth may know that you alone, O LORD, are God. (2 Kings 19:19)

Arise, O LORD! Deliver me, O my God! Strike all my enemies on the jaw; break the teeth of the wicked. (Psalm 3:7)

I sought the LORD, and he answered me; he delivered me from all my fears. (Psalm 34:4)

He has delivered me from all my troubles, and my eyes have looked in triumph on my foes. (Psalm 54:7)

You have delivered me from death and my feet from stumbling, that I may walk before God in the light of life. (Psalm 56:13)

Deliver me from my enemies, O God; protect me from those who rise up against me. Deliver me from evildoers and save me from bloodthirsty men. (Psalm 59:1–2)

Deliver me, O my God, from the hand of the wicked, from the grasp of evil and cruel men. (Psalm 71:4)

Help us, O God our Savior, for the glory of your name; deliver us and forgive our sins for your name's sake. (Psalm 79:9)

Lead us not into temptation, but deliver us from the evil one. (Matthew 6:13)

He has delivered us from such a deadly peril, and he will deliver us. On him we have set our hope that he will continue to deliver us. (2 Corinthians 1:10)

These verses clearly demonstrate the feelings of people who felt that when their backs were to the wall, they could call out to the Lord, knowing He would deliver them. In preparation for writing this book, I researched both the Old and the New Testaments. I did not find one verse that described a scenario where God refused to help those who called on His name for freedom.

What does this mean for us? It means that we can count on this wonderful biblical principle: God liberates the oppressed and sets the captive free. He will break the evil strongholds that try to oppress us. He will help us overcome our vices, addictions, fears, and anxieties. He will help us overcome the power of sin that lures us to compromise what we know is right and godly.

Do you feel stuck, bound, or find yourself fighting an uphill battle against overwhelming temptations? Do you struggle with a difficult vice such as compulsive spending, drug addiction, pornography, or alcoholism? Perhaps your addiction to sugar has kept your eating in a vicious cycle. Whatever the emotional or spiritual opposition, the following prayer is a biblical way of asking God to initiate freedom in your life. I encourage you to pray this prayer—or one that you can put in your own words—at least once a day. I believe you will experience a significant breakthrough as a result. Be sure to write down the answer when God responds.

The Prayer for Freedom

Lord, I am surrounded by an enemy that seeks to devour me. I want to do what is right, but when I try, I wind up doing the very thing I tried to avoid. I need Your strength. I need Your power. I need Your mighty hand to deliver me. Break the chains the enemy has placed on my life. Set me free from all that entangles me and all that seeks to destroy me. Show me Your door to freedom and give me the strength to walk through it. Fill me with Your peace in the midst of my anxiety. Deliver me this day. In Christ's name I pray, amen.

This prayer can greatly benefit your personal life, or it can address the broader issues that your family faces. Either way, God responds to the petition of those who seek His help. While this prayer asks God for help in a general way, you may need His help in a specific area. If so, I have outlined five distinct ways you can apply the prayer for freedom, including freedom from diabolical oppression; vices and addictions; fear and anxiety; the power of sin; and over money, power, and fame. I have adapted the prayer for freedom to address each of those specific areas.

The following pages will give you some powerful insights on how to experience freedom through prayer. As we focus on the five areas that impact people the most, the only thing we need in order to experience God's power is a desire to be free and a genuine heart.

II. How the Prayer for Freedom Can Help You Experience Power in Five Crucial Areas of Your Life

1. Experiencing Freedom from Diabolical Oppression

Over the centuries, Satan has succeeded in convincing different civilizations that he doesn't exist. This is becoming particularly true in Western culture. Unfortunately, evil exists, and our enemy has a mission. He has imparted that mission to the diabolical forces that work with him. Together they seek to bring devastation to all that God deems valuable, beautiful, and worthy. You and I are at the center of the battle that is waged between the kingdom of God and the kingdom of darkness (1 John 3:8). We are not casualties of war, nor are we caught in the cross fire. Instead, we are the prizes, and we are the ones who determine which side wins (2 Cor. 10:4–5). For God, you are His cherished and beloved child with whom He wants to spend eternity. For Satan, you represent a mere hunting trophy that he wants to hang over his mantel. The apostle Peter describes our adversary well: "Be self-controlled and alert. Your enemy the devil prowls around like a roaring lion looking for someone to devour" (1 Pet. 5:8).

Satan tempts and oppresses everyone—believers and nonbelievers alike. He comes to the door of our hearts and knocks in search of an inroad. James understood the importance of resisting temptation: "Submit yourselves, then, to God. Resist the devil, and he will flee from you" (James 4:7). He also gave us a stern warning of the consequences of opening the door to temptation: "Each one is tempted when, by his own evil desire, he is dragged away and enticed. Then, after desire has conceived, it gives birth to sin;

and sin, when it is full-grown, gives birth to death" (James 1:14–15).

When people give in to temptation and continue to grant the enemy access to their hearts, he establishes a foothold. At that point, from a secure place, he can torment and manipulate them and does so whenever he chooses. That is one reason why people find it difficult to break their addiction to mood-altering substances, illicit sexual experiences, and certain types of unethical behavior (compulsive lying, corruption, and stealing). People, in essence, give the enemy permission to operate freely in an area of their lives. In addition, people who are filled with rage, carry grudges, or find it difficult to forgive others can become tormented as well. That is why Paul wrote, "'In your anger do not sin': Do not let the sun go down while you are still angry, and do not give the devil a foothold" (Eph. 4:26).

A few years back, we toured Central America holding citywide crusades with two enormous tents. One had a seating capacity of five thousand. We used the other tent as a counseling and spiritual deliverance center where hundreds of people came and talked with counselors each night. It was surprising to see so many ordinary middle-class people who faced spiritual issues that I thought existed only in the New Testament. We helped people who suffered unbelievable amounts of anguish, including those who were tormented and even possessed by demons. There were some who occasionally attended a religious service and there were others who wouldn't darken the doors of a local church.

One night a man parked his vehicle in the dirt lot adjacent to our tents. He looked weary and fatigued and had various lesions on his face. During the music, he showed no emotion. During the message, he was expressionless. Toward the end of the altar call, I made the announcement, "If you feel trapped as if something is holding you back, we have counselors who are ready to talk with you." About 120 people, including the young man, stood to their feet and followed an usher, who escorted them from the large tent to the other.

When the young man walked through the door, his anxiety level increased significantly. When he sat down in front of the lay minister, he squirmed in his seat. The counselor leaned forward slightly and asked, "Hello, friend. What is your name?" Wringing his hands he replied, "Jeremiah." "Well Jeremiah, my name is Robert. How can I help you tonight?"

"It's these voices," he said. "Each night they tell me that the only way to experience peace is to end it all." "You mean 'kill yourself,'?" Robert interjected. Jeremiah paused. "Yes. I want to make it all go away. I just want to stop the craziness!" Then he began to intensely claw his face with his fingernails until he was bleeding. Robert looked at him with compassion. "Oh, don't do that," he said. Then he grabbed some tissue and dipped it in a cup of water. Leaning over, he put one hand around Jeremiah's shoulders and used the other to wipe the blood from Jeremiah's face. Then he began to pray softly.

After a few minutes Robert said, "First of all, Jeremiah, this is a safe place. Nothing can harm you here. Second, the God of the universe wants to help end your torment. He wants to help you break free."

"Why are you being so kind to me?" Jeremiah asked. "You don't even know me."

"You are not here by chance. God loves you and considers you His child. Who am I to treat you differently?" Robert replied.

Jeremiah began to feel somewhat at ease. He went on to explain that his father was very abusive. His mother stood silently on the sidelines and refused to intervene. His past was filled with pain and broken dreams. He had hoped that when he moved out on his own everything would change. Unfortunately, time doesn't heal all.

Robert opened his Bible and began to share some critical things that Jeremiah needed to hear. "Christ's mission," Robert said, "is to set the captive free." Then he read Acts 10:38: "God anointed Jesus of Nazareth with the Holy Spirit and power, and...he went around doing good and healing all who were under the power of the devil, because God was with him." He closed his Bible and looked Jeremiah in the eye and said, "The Lord will set you free, if you desire."

With tears in his eyes, Jeremiah responded, "Yes. That's what I want more than anything." That night, Jeremiah discovered the importance of recuperating his will to live. When I saw his transformation through their time of talking, reading, and praying, I was reminded of a similar story found in the Gospel of Mark.

The shadowy figure had supernatural strength that overpowered anyone who tried to subdue him. The people of the town were terrified. They tried to bind his hands and feet with irons, but he broke the chains as if they were made of plastic. Night and day, he wandered through the tombs on the side of the hill and cut himself with jagged rocks. Indeed, the diabolical forces wanted to take his life. Perhaps that was why they drove him to the cemetery.

One day, Jesus arrived at the shore in a boat. When the

man saw Him from a distance, he ran and fell at His feet. Knowing what drove the man, Jesus raised His voice and said, "Come out of him!" The man shouted back, "What do You want with me, Jesus, Son of the Most High God? Swear to God that You won't torture me!" This was like nothing Jesus had seen before in His years of ministry.

Jesus asked him, "What is your name?" "Legion," the voice exclaimed, "for we are many!" Not just one demon or even ten possessed the man. More than two thousand demons were torturing him. But the Lord discovered the crack in their armor. Their greatest fear was being cast into the Abyss. So they implored Him to let them move from their position of dominion in the man's soul to a herd of two thousand pigs pasturing nearby. Jesus granted their request. As soon as the legion of demons entered the pigs, they exploded down an embankment and drowned in the lake. There was little doubt of their diabolical intention. They planned on killing the man all along.

Those who were tending the pigs spread the word throughout the region about everything that had happened. When they came and saw the man dressed and in his right mind, instead of celebrating, they were afraid. (Story paraphrased from Mark 5 NIV.)

Several things stand out in these two stories of Jeremiah and the demon-possessed man. First, no one is ever too far gone. There is hope for everyone, no matter how dire the circumstance. Second, regardless of how terrible things get, people can always maintain a small portion of their will and reclaim the rest whenever they choose. The man who was driven by the legion of demons retained enough sense to recognize his only solution when he saw it. Then he ran without stopping until he reached Him. Third, all demonic forces obey Christ's orders. As long as our hearts are truly aligned with God's, we can live with the assurance that we live under the protection of the Lord and Master of all creation, "for he has rescued us from the dominion of darkness and brought us into the kingdom of the Son he loves" (Col. 1:13). The keys to our freedom are not in God's hands alone. We share the responsibility with Him. We must take the first step by turning to God through prayer and resisting the devil. We must use the authority that God has given us to stand firm.

You may not feel that your life is in the same condition as the lives of the two people I just mentioned, and I hope it isn't. Regardless of your circumstances, though, Christ has the power to set you free. The only thing you need is the common sense to recognize that He is your solution.

If you feel tormented by diabolical forces, if you cannot find peace, if something is trying to steal your will to live, if there is an impending doom that constantly hovers over your head, if you have inadvertently opened the door too many times to the enemy, I want you to take a few moments to meditate on the Scripture verses below. The prayer that follows the verses is very similar to the one that Jeremiah— and thousands of others—prayed when he experienced his breakthrough in our crusade.

In all these things we are more than conquerors through him who loved us. For I am convinced that neither death nor life, neither angels nor demons, neither the present nor the future, nor any powers, neither height nor depth, nor anything else in all creation, will be able to separate us from the love of God that is in Christ Jesus our Lord. (Romans 8:37–39)

Lord, I feel oppressed and surrounded by diabolical forces. I call on Your name, because I believe that You will respond to my request. Cleanse me of all sin, and create a clean heart in me. I ask You to silence the voice of the enemy so I can hear Your voice and follow Your clear direction to freedom. I resist the attacks that come against me, and I say "Be gone" to the destructive forces that try to bring about my demise. I resist their destructive thoughts, and I reclaim my will to live the life that Christ has purposed me to live.

Lord, I open my heart and receive Your power, Your strength, Your healing, and Your peace right now. Deliver me this day from the hand of the enemy. In Christ's name I pray, amen.

2. Experiencing Freedom from Vices and Addictions

I turned on the television while we were living in Costa Rica a few years back. Billy Graham stood on a platform in the middle of a large stadium and said, "You might be addicted to drugs or alcohol, but you can be delivered by the power of God." The evangelist was right. There isn't a stronghold, vice, addiction, or sinful pattern that God can't break. And no one is exempt from the potential of experiencing a powerful breakthrough. In my years of ministry, I have seen many people make significant breakthroughs. I would like to share one in particular as a powerful example.

Deborah was daddy's little girl, but when he had an affair and decided to leave the family, it was devastating. She was sixteen years old. The divorce was ugly, and as a result, she and her mother had to sell the house. The anger and bitterness stayed with her for years.

After trying to finish her college degree, she eventually gave up. It seemed that for each step forward she took one step backward. In her early twenties, she became a social drinker and enjoyed the nightlife in local clubs. The liquid courage helped her overcome her shyness and become more outgoing. But after turning thirty, she started to withdraw from her friends.

She no longer went to nightclubs, and loneliness and depression set in. In order to silence the haunting voices of anxiety, pain, and frustration, she turned to her old companion that never abandoned her. She began to drink with greater frequency.

For more than a decade her vice grew, and with it her bout with depression. Many nights, she cried herself to sleep asking God to end her life. Fortunately, He refused to answer her prayer. At the beginning of 2009, she reached the end of her rope. She dropped to her knees, cried out to God, and asked Him to take control of her life. That winter night changed everything.

It didn't happen in one day or in six months. But eventually, God broke the paralyzing chains of alcoholism over her life. Although she knew Christ and discovered God's purpose for living, she still struggled with the addiction. On the morning after her forty-fourth birthday celebration, she looked at the ceiling of the hospital room where she lay with tears in her eyes. The excessive drinking the night before was too much for her body to handle. She could no longer ignore God's still, small voice that urged her to put down the bottle. In the same way she cried out to God the year before when facing the diabolical voices of suicide, she asked Him to help her break the chains of addiction.

That morning, God began something miraculous in Deborah. It's an ongoing miracle that continues to this day. She hasn't had a drop of alcohol since that time.

Indeed, God opens doors for anyone who wants to be free. He liberates the oppressed and breaks the chains upon those who are caught in bondage. There is no addiction too great. There is no vice too powerful. There is no sinful pattern too overwhelming. There is no stronghold that can resist the power of God. Jesus proclaimed this message of hope: "The Spirit of the Lord is on me, because he has anointed me to preach good news to the poor. He has sent me to proclaim freedom for the prisoners and recovery of sight for the blind, to release the oppressed, to proclaim the year of the Lord's favor" (Luke 4:18–19).

If you struggle with a vice, eating disorder, compulsive behavior, addiction, or sinful pattern that you've never been able to overcome, God offers you His power to change. He understands your disappointments, your frustrations, and your pain. Throughout the New Testament, Christ is recognized unequivocally as the deliverer who came to set the captive free. The following prayer can help you during your struggle to find the freedom you desire:

Lord, I receive Your power to overcome the vices and addictions that have kept me bound. Fill me with Your strength and give me Your discipline to follow through on what is wise, healthy, and good. Forgive me for allowing my heart to become attached to these destructive patterns. I ask You to break the chains the enemy has placed on me, and grant me the freedom that only You can give. In Christ's name I pray, amen.

3. Experiencing Freedom from Fear, Worry, and Anxiety

I have yet to meet someone who didn't want peace. I'm quite sure that as you lie down at night and rest your head on your pillow, you long to put the busyness and frustrations of your day behind you. Yet when all the noise ceases and the rest of the world comes to a standstill, you may find it difficult to slow your mind down. Perhaps it's difficult to push back the anxiety and worry you face. During such times of heavy concern, you don't need another drink. You don't need an escape. You need God's peace.

God's peace is the opposite of fear and anxiety. Like His love, it is greater than anything we can comprehend. Paul summed it up when he said, "Do not be anxious about anything, but in everything, by prayer and petition, with thanksgiving, present your requests to God. And the peace of God, which transcends all understanding, will guard your hearts and your minds in Christ Jesus" (Phil. 4:6–7).

Satan, on the other hand, knows what people want but cannot offer them genuine peace. Instead, he must offer cheap imitations. That is why people turn to mood-altering substances such as alcohol or drugs. However, such experiences are nothing more than an inferior, less effective version of God's peace.

Peace in the Midst of a Violent Storm

Imagine you are on a cross-country flight. Suddenly the

plane flies through an area of moderate turbulence. The pilot makes an announcement and tells the flight attendants to be seated until the weather clears up. Within minutes, however, the pockets of turbulence become violent as the 737 falls and rises at the whim of the surrounding storm. The passengers squeeze their armrests, close their eyes, and clench their teeth. Even the flight attendants are noticeably concerned about their safety. Deep down inside you begin to wonder if the structural integrity of the aircraft is not in question. Without warning, the cockpit door flies open and the pilots run out screaming, "We're going down! We're falling out of the sky!" I am not sure how you would feel, but something similar happened to Jesus one afternoon.

He was crossing the lake with His disciples after a long day. He was exhausted. So as they left the shore, He went to the back of the boat and lay down on a cushion. Within minutes, He fell asleep. Suddenly a large storm developed and began to overwhelm the boat. The disciples were experienced fishermen and had navigated their way through many difficult storms, but there was something different about this tempest. The waves were crashing over the bow and filled the boat to the point of sinking. They panicked.

They ran to the back and shook Him out of His sleep. "Master, Master, we're going to drown!" He opened His eyes in a startle, looked around, and quickly stood to His feet. Looking toward the front of the boat, He rebuked the wind and the raging waters. Immediately the wind stopped and the lake flattened out. Within seconds, everything was calm.

He briefly closed His eyes, exhaled through His nostrils,

and turned to His disciples. "Where is your faith?" He asked them. They had no answer. Instead, they were filled with another type of fear, the fear of God. They whispered to one another, "Who is this man? Even the wind and the waves obey him!" (Story paraphrased from Mark 4:35–41 NIV.)

Jesus fell asleep because He was tired, and because He knew He was getting to the other side. His peace allowed Him to rest, even though He knew He was heading into a storm. In many ways, we are like the disciples. Our faith in God should give us the security of knowing that we will get to the other side. Unfortunately, we allow our intimidating circumstances to determine whether we rest or fret, whether we have peace or anxiety.

For a long time beginning when I was a child, I was constantly fidgety and restless. Although my mom allowed me to play the drums, baseball, hockey, and work my way through high school, I still had tons of energy. My mom could always tell how nervous I was at any given moment, depending on how short my fingernails were.

In 2005, my wife and girls and I were two months from moving from Central America back to the United States. We were concerned about the logistics of the move. We were concerned about the financial pressure. We were concerned about how our daughters were going to adapt to a new school in a country that had changed dramatically since the attacks on September 11. I finally came to the conclusion that I needed God to deliver me from the worries that I allowed to swirl around in my heart.

For one month I sat on the couch during my devotions and used Psalm 23 as a prayer. Every day, I changed the words of the psalm to apply to the areas of my personal life and the issues I was facing. Within a week, I noticed that my head was clear. I didn't feel on edge. After two weeks, I noticed something else. For the first time in thirty-eight years, I had fingernails. I went two weeks without biting my nails. For the last six years, I have used a nail clipper. God helped me overcome my generalized anxiety and fear. The place that was once occupied by my worries, He filled with His peace.

Now more than ever, people need God's peace. The mother needs God's peace in regard to the well-being of her children. The homeowner needs God's peace in regard to his real-estate investment. The elderly woman needs God's peace in regard to her health. The student needs God's peace regarding her future career. The businessman needs God's peace in regard to the economy.

If you are plagued by worry, fear, and anxiety, "trust in the LORD with all your heart and lean not on your own understanding" (Prov. 3:5). If you feel overwhelmed by what lurks around the corner determined to destroy you, just remember, "The LORD himself goes before you and will be with you; he will never leave you nor forsake you. Do not be afraid; do not be discouraged" (Deut. 31:8). If you are concerned about your financial well-being, your health, your career, or your future, remember that Christ said, "The very hairs of your head are all numbered" (Luke 12:7). When the intimidating voice of oppression threatens you, stand firm and lift up the prayer for freedom. You will see the hand of God move in your life.

The following prayer can help you draw close to the Lord in times of fear and anxiety. Open your heart and ask God to fill you with His peace.

THE PRAYER FOR FREEDOM

Lord, I ask You to rebuke the storm that is slamming into my life. Deliver me from the hand of the enemy that seeks to fill me with fear. I do not want to feel overwhelmed with anxiety. I want to experience Your presence, strength, and power. I open my heart to You and receive Your peace that supersedes all fear and worry. I resist the anxiety that the enemy is using to intimidate me, and I proclaim that every aspect of my life is in God's hands. In Christ's name I pray, amen.

4. Experiencing Freedom from the Power of Sin

Sin separates us from God and prevents us from having a blessed life. If we don't tap into the power of God, sin can shatter our lives, destroy our families, and do something even worse. It can change our final destiny and determine where we spend eternity. Some people might say, "If Christ has forgiven us, we are clean in God's eyes." This is true. However, there is a significant difference between someone who is *forgiven* and someone who is *truly free*. We can be forgiven from a life of sin, but we still need the power of God to deliver us from the power of sin.

I will never forget the conversation I had with the pastor of a church in Latin America. We were two days from the commencement of our citywide crusade in the baseball stadium. The pastor said, "Jason, we are glad you are here, and we believe that God will do many powerful things in our city. But I am concerned about the term 'freedom.'" I asked, "What would be your concern?" He replied, "I believe that when people believe that Christ is the Savior, He forgives them of their sin. Therefore, you don't need to keep talking about freedom or deliverance, because we are made whole in Christ when we believe."

I knew his heart and wanted to treat him with the upmost respect, especially in front of his colleagues. I said to him, "I understand your conviction. I really do. But tell me, have you ever disciplined a board member for sleeping around or for spreading rumors behind your back? Have you ever caught an usher trying to steal money out of the offering? Have you ever dealt with a youth leader who was watching porn on a church computer? How many members of your church continue to struggle in their battle against the power of sin?" His silence said it all. Freedom from the power of sin implies that Jesus is not only our Savior, but also Lord of our lives.

I wish it weren't true, but 62 percent of the people who come into our crusade counseling center with spiritual and emotional bondages have some sort of affiliation with a local church. Christians need the power of God just as much as non-Christians in order to be free from the power of sin.

5. Experiencing Freedom over Money, Power, and Fame

The man signed the papers and collected the payment for the sale of his lot. Without hesitation, he made his way directly to Solomon's Colonnade. When his friends saw him, they welcomed him with open arms. At the far end of the meeting room sat several of the apostles. "Come in, Barnabas," Peter said.

"I sold some land, and this is all the money from the sale of the property." Barnabas leaned down in front of Peter and laid the money at his feet. "This is for the Lord's work." The group of believers appreciated his gesture and blessed him for his contribution. But deep down inside, Ananias and his wife, Sapphira, felt jealous of the attention Barnabas received from the leaders of the church.

Ananias went out and sold some land, and with the full knowledge of his wife, kept a portion of the proceeds. It was theirs to do with as they saw fit. That was their justification. Then he brought the rest to Peter. "We sold some land, and this is the money from the sale of the property." Peter paused for a moment, looked him in the eye, and said, "Ananias, how is it that Satan has so filled your heart that you have lied to the Holy Spirit and have kept for yourself some of the money you received for the land? Didn't it belong to you before it was sold? And after it was sold, wasn't the money at your disposal? What made you think of doing such a thing? You have not lied to men but to God." The motive to sell the property wasn't to bless the church. Both he and his wife sold the property to gain a reputation for greater generosity than they merited.[1] In the same way that Achan died because he kept a portion of the spoils for himself, Ananias was guilty of the same sin. Upon hearing Peter's words, he dropped dead at the apostle's feet.

Without hesitation, a few of the younger men wrapped his body and buried him. The fear of God fell upon the members of the community that heard about the tragedy. His wife came to meet with the apostles three hours later but had no knowledge of what had happened to her husband. Peter could have mentioned her husband's death, but he didn't. He had sufficient time to ponder what took place earlier that day. So instead, he asked her about the sale of the property. "Tell me, is this the price you and Ananias got for the land?" "Yes," she said, "that is the price." Peter said to her, "How could you agree to test the Spirit of the Lord? Look! The feet of the men who buried your husband are at the door, and they will carry you out also." The couple did what was wrong. It was sin, and they knew it. Their sinful nature tried to buy them influence among the believers, but instead, the power of sin wound up killing them. Upon hearing Peter's words, Sapphira dropped dead. (Story paraphrased from Acts 4:34–5:10 NIV.)

Deceiving men is one thing, but trying to deceive the Spirit of God is something else altogether. Only the power of sin could drive them to walk such a fine line and lure them into lying to God. Ironically, they lost their lives over something serious but of little importance. The couple failed to tap into the power of God that could have liberated them from what kept them bound. Like many, it was their love of money, thirst for power, and the lust for notoriety that led to their downfall.

In what ways are you walking a fine line? In what ways does the power of sin keep you bound? In what ways does it lure you into believing that you can fool others and even God? Are you guilty of something you know isn't right? If the power of sin is taking its toll on you, and you cannot seem to gain victory, the Lord will deliver you from its oppressive grip. When you cannot see the light at the end of the tunnel, call out to God. His grace and strength will be more than sufficient to help you break the dominion of sin over your life.

Because of the power of God, we no longer have to be held captive to the power of sin (1 John 5:18; Rom. 6:6). If you want to be free, lift up the following prayer with sincerity. Make sure there is nothing in your heart that is disingenuous, and the hand of God will move powerfully in your life.

> Lord, I do not want to be a slave to the power of sin. I do not want any sinful pattern to exist in my life. I want You to set me free. Break every sinful pattern and release me from the dominion of sin over my life. Give me the ability to recognize any impure motive and the strength to do what is right in Your eyes. I open my heart and receive Your life-transforming power. In Christ's name I pray, amen.

III. Discovering Power in Your Time of Need

You Are a Candidate for Transformation

Recently, I spoke at a prison. After I concluded my message, a young Hispanic man came up to the chain-link fence that separated us. He was dressed in an orange jumpsuit and had a scar across his forehead. With tears streaming down his face he said, "I've made so many mistakes. I'm only eighteen, but this is the second time I've been arrested for doing drugs. Do you think there is hope for me to change? Do you think that Christ can set me free?" I said, "Without a doubt, I know that the Lord is the solution that you need today!" He said, "I am such a disappointment to my mom. She loves me and prays for me. And, what can I say? Here I am." Then he just sobbed. I said, "God is all-powerful and specializes in putting lives back together. You, my friend, are no exception to that fact. You have some tough choices to make, but if you are sincere, God will lead you out of the storm." Then we prayed a prayer similar to the one that I outlined above.

Several months later, a chaplain contacted me. He said, "Jason, I received a communication from one of the inmates that you prayed with at the end of your presentation. He said that God has helped him overcome his addiction. Since leaving prison, he has been clean and sober and is grateful for all the Lord has done in his life."

No vice, addiction, destructive pattern, or spiritual opposition is too difficult for God. Everyone is a candidate for transformation.

Time Is Irrelevant

Some people think that the longer someone is sick, the more the condition becomes a part of his or her identity. Many feel the same way about spiritual oppression, addictions, and dysfunctional behavior—that when it becomes a part of a person's identity, it is that much harder to break. This is simply not true. In light of what God's power can do when we pray, anyone can experience His breakthrough. Why? Because to God, time is irrelevant.

When Christ asked His disciples, "What are you arguing about?" a man spoke up and said, "Teacher, I brought my son, who is possessed by a spirit that has robbed him of speech. Whenever it seizes him, it throws him to the ground. He foams at the mouth, gnashes his teeth, and becomes rigid. I asked your disciples to drive out the spirit, but they could not."

After expressing frustration with His followers, Jesus called for the boy. As soon as the spirit saw Jesus, it threw the boy violently to the ground, and he started to convulse. Foaming at the mouth, he rolled around uncontrollably.

Jesus turned to the boy's father and asked, "How long has he been like this?" He replied, "Ever since he was a child. A spirit seizes him and often throws him into fire or water in an effort to kill him. Please, if You can do anything, I beg You, help us."

"What do you mean, 'If You can?' What kind of a question is that? Everything is possible for him who believes," Jesus responded. The boy's father cried out, "I want to believe. I really do. But please help me overcome my unbelief!"

Jesus turned to the boy and rebuked the evil spirit. "You deaf and mute spirit," He said, "I command you, come out of him and never enter him again." The spirit shook the boy violently and shrieked loudly. Then suddenly, the evil spirit left him. There he lay, completely still. Some wondered if the spirit had killed him, but Jesus bent down, took him by the hand, and lifted him to his feet. The boy looked around, and to the amazement of everyone, came to his senses.

The disciples pulled their Master aside and asked, "Why couldn't we drive it out?" He replied, "This kind can come out only by prayer." (Story paraphrased from Mark 9:16–29 NIV.)

The years had taken an emotional toll on the boy's father. The evil spirit obviously became a part of the boy's identity. Even the disciples seemed to be somewhat perplexed. But the amount of time the boy was subject to the evil spirit had no effect on God's power. Whether you have struggled with something for a day or twenty years, remember, time is irrelevant to God. It's relevant only to you.

How to Break Free from the Traps of Life

A few months ago, I heard small creatures scurrying around in my attic. The nuisance started at 3:00 a.m. and lasted a couple of hours. After the second night, I called the property management company of our homeowners association and explained that Ratatouille had moved in and opened an after-hours nightclub.

That afternoon, the exterminator came. The young expert smiled when I opened the door and said, "I hear you've got rat problems." "Yes, I do," I replied. "Let's take a look in your attic," he said.

At first glance, he didn't think there was much evidence of rat traffic. "I can leave a few traps up here and come back in a week and check." "That would be fine," I replied. We set four industrial rattraps and closed the attic door.

Sure enough, at 3:00 a.m. I heard movement just above my head. It sounded like the rat was chewing his way through the ceiling. Fortunately, that didn't happen. Instead, I heard a loud *thump* in the same area where we had set one of the traps. It was just above the attic door.

Then nothing. Just silence.

Hallelujah, I thought. *My nightmare is finally over, and I can go back to sleep.*

Within five minutes, I heard a disturbing noise coming from the same area. It sounded like Ratatouille had found a baseball bat and started to club the plywood like a caveman. I got up and walked into our closet and stood under the attic door. I quietly closed the closet door and opened the ladder in slow motion. Tiptoeing up the ladder, I slowly pushed up on the attic door in an effort to make the rat retreat. As soon as I touched the door, *Bam!* The rat slammed whatever it possessed down onto the door. *Forget that!* I said to myself. *I may weigh 180 pounds and stand over six-two, but I think it would be prudent to wait until the exterminator comes tomorrow.*

For the next three hours, the rat wouldn't let anyone sleep. At 8:00 a.m., I called the exterminators again and told them to send the bravest officer on the force. Within thirty minutes, the doorbell rang. The same smile greeted me when I opened the door. "I hear they're back," he said. "Yes they are," I replied. I explained everything that had happened the night before. "I'll take care of it." I said, "I don't know. If the rat had a gun, I'm sure he would use it." "Seriously, don't worry," he said confidently.

He placed the ladder under the attic door, climbed up the steps, and pushed up. *Bam!* The rat responded with the same force as before. "AHHHHHHHH!" the tall, 220-pound exterminator screamed—like an eight-year-old girl. I smiled and said, "I told you so." His voice quivered: "I'm not sure what to do." I said, "Sure you do. That why we're paying you the big bucks!" Between the two of us, we weighed more than four hundred pounds and measured more than twelve feet tall. Yet a creature that weighed less than a pound held us hostage.

After taking thirty seconds to regain his composure, he mustered up the courage to try again. He lifted the attic door at an angle in order to slide the rat away from the opening. The rat continued its noisy protest. The exterminator stood the door upright, preventing the rat from leaping down into the closet. He flipped on the light, paused for a second, and said, "I've never seen anything like this in my life." "What is it?" I asked. "You need to come up here and see this." I replied, "Uh, I'm not so sure that's a good idea." "No, it's safe," he assured me.

I proceeded to climb the ladder and entered the attic. I slowly glanced over the top of the attic door that served as my only shield of protection. There the rat sat. He was caught in the trap, but for some reason, his neck did not snap. Instead, he walked around, carrying the trap and slamming it into different things trying to free himself. He wasn't in pain, but he was mad. Fortunately for us, he couldn't go anywhere very fast.

That morning, a powerful yet somewhat flawed spiritual analogy came to me. Like the rat stuck in the trap, many people get caught in the trap of a vice, addiction, or destructive pattern. The cheese of temptation lures them, and before they know it, their freedom is gone. They are captives. Unfortunately, they spend the rest of their lives carrying the weight of their traps, flopping around trying to free themselves, but they wind up making things worse in the process.

If you've tried to free yourself from whatever keeps you in bondage but your efforts have failed every time, call out to the Lord. He will hear your prayer and give you freedom from the dominion of evil. In your darkest hour when no one seems to understand much less care, God does. He sees your heart, understands your struggle, and is willing to do everything necessary to escort you to a life of freedom.

Finally, I want to highlight something that Jesus shared with His disciples. When He taught them to pray, He gave them the Lord's Prayer as a model to communicate with God. He felt that it should be a significant part of their prayer lives, because it had deep spiritual relevance for every human being. Christ knew that when His followers genuinely expressed its words, the Father would answer. The final portion of His prayer deals with the concept of freedom and overcoming the forces of darkness.

It reads: "Lead us not into temptation, but deliver us from the evil one" (Matt. 6:13). Christ knows that it is God's perfect will to empower us to overcome temptation and deliver us from evil. Why would He instruct the disciples to pray in such a way if it were not God's will or if God had no intention of answering the prayer? Leading us away from temptation and delivering us from evil is something we can always count on God to do.

What gives me the authority to say that God always answers the prayer for freedom? Because Christ's mission statement found in Luke 4:18–19 and Acts 10:38 clearly states that He came to set the captive free. His purpose was to save, redeem, and deliver all who were in need. And today, every breathing human being is a candidate to receive this wonderful gift. You, my friend, are not an exception to that fact. So when you ask the Lord to give you freedom, you can expect Him to answer that prayer! *He is your deliverer.*

As we reflect upon this chapter, I hope you are convinced that God loves you and will help you overcome the spiritual oppression that holds you back. Regardless of the vices, anxieties, or strongholds that have plagued your life, the Lord will complete the work He began in you (Phil. 1:6).

If you have felt that for every step forward you've taken a step backward, I know how frustrating it can be. I know how emotionally exhausting it is when you can't find peace, when you feel anxious about your life, or when you don't know what tomorrow brings. During those times, try to remember to "cast all your anxiety on him because he cares for you" (1 Pet. 5:7). Allow the Prince of Peace to push back the storms of your life and calm the anxieties of your heart. I am fully confident that He will answer your prayer for freedom.

All the prayers for freedom listed in this chapter can be summed up with this simple prayer: *Lord, set me free, and break the chains in my life.*

The Prayer for Provision

G eorge, I am not sure how to say this, but I think our
missionary career is over," I struggled to say. "What
do you mean, 'over'?" my friend and former pastor asked.
"I don't see any way around this mountain." I couldn't believe that after overcoming so many challenges, we had no
choice but to go home. I was devastated. When he asked
how we had come to our decision, I found it difficult to articulate the words.

Three years prior, I was selling paper for a Fortune 500
corporation. Cindee was an executive assistant for a mergers and acquisitions company. We felt the call to leave our
decent-paying jobs and become missionaries in Latin America. So we requested an application from our denomination
headquarters. They resisted sending it to us, because we
owed thousands of dollars in school loans. When I called
George Wood, who was our district assistant superintendent at the time, he said, "Jason, let me see what I can do."
Fifteen minutes later, he called me back. "They're sending

you the application today." I have no idea what he said, but I'm fairly confident that his having been our pastor helped significantly.

For the next year and a half, Cindee and I worked hard, lived in a trailer, and paid off all but $2,500 in school loans. We made great progress.

Finally, the day came. Cindee and I sat in our final interview one year after we'd filled out the application. Across the table sat the regional directors for each of the continents of the globe. The executive director leaned back in his chair and said, "Jason, I hope you understand that becoming a missionary isn't just a mere career change. We continue the work that started two thousand years ago. As missionaries, what we do and who we are is directly connected to the church in the book of Acts. So before you think that this is simply a nice change from corporate America, I hope you understand the severity and profound consequences of this decision." I didn't try to give an eloquent reply. All I said was, "I will do my best to reach people for Christ."

After our interviews, we set out to raise our budget during the economic recession of the early nineties. When we arrived in Costa Rica, I embarked upon the most difficult portion of the entire process, language school. I spent a full year studying vocabulary, phonetics, grammar, and basic conversation. Somehow, we overcame several tragedies that year, including the death of my stepfather, my dad's heart attack, and a major traffic accident. The end of language school signified that I had *made it*. After three years of hard work, difficult transition, and strenuous preparation, we were ready to begin our ministry overseas.

That's when everything came to a grinding halt.

Cindee grew up speaking Spanish as a missionary kid in

Latin America. She didn't need to attend language school. Nonetheless, our first year in Costa Rica was extremely challenging for her. She struggled with depression. We had an eighteen-month-old baby and another one on the way. Many nights, she cried herself to sleep. Other times, she just lay on the bathroom floor for hours.

We called one of the missionary counselors in the United States. After talking with Cindee for five minutes, he said to me, "I suggest that you bring your wife to our counseling center. She is suffering from moderate depression and needs help. I am sure that being seven months pregnant isn't helping either."

Within a week, we headed to Emerge Ministries in Akron, Ohio, where my wife met with a counselor for seven weeks.

One night, when our daughter was fast asleep, I asked Cindee to sit down at the kitchen table in our rented apartment. I could tell that she felt conflicted about returning to Costa Rica. She was trying her best to work things out, and that's all that mattered. I took her hand in mine and looked into her beautiful brown eyes and said, "If we have to move back to California, then that's what we'll do. If I have to sell paper again, then that's what I will do. We can serve the Lord anywhere. I just want you to know that you are more important to me than moving back to Costa Rica."

I am not sure what exactly resonated with her, but in a matter of days, she felt a conviction that it was worth another attempt. She said, "I'm ready to go back to the country where we believe the Lord wants us to work."

There was one final obstacle that I had been reluctant to tackle. As missionaries-in-training, our salary was half that of established missionaries. Our salary was set up for living in Central America, not for living on the road in the United States. As a result, we accumulated new debt living three months in Akron in addition to flying home for my stepfather's funeral.

There was no way to survive on our $8,000-a-year salary and make our minimum monthly payments. After sitting down and figuring out a new budget, I knew that we were $5,000 short. When I laid down the pencil, I sat back in my chair in disbelief. *It's all going to end because of five grand*, I thought.

This time, I couldn't work my way out of the mess.

During our time at Emerge Ministries, I stayed in contact with George. Since he was the one who initially convinced our denomination to send us the missionary application, I felt I needed to call him with our final update.

"Hello, Jason. How is Cindee feeling?" he asked. "Cindee is doing very well," I replied. "Thank you for being a good friend to us. Listen, George, I called because, well, I am not sure how to say this, but I think our missionary career is over." "What do you mean, 'over'?" "I don't see any way out," I said.

He listened intently as I summarized the story. Then he said, "Something has come up. Let me call you back in a few minutes." His position had many demands. So I knew he had other pressing issues. About fifteen minutes went by, and the phone rang again. He said, "Jason, I have a check in my hand with your name on it. It's for $5,000. Will this help?"

It seemed someone in our district years before had the foresight to set up an emergency fund for missionaries, and the amount in the account was exactly what we needed. After the birth of our second daughter, Chanel, we returned to Costa Rica and within eighteen months started an international crusade ministry that continues today. God provided exactly what we needed. As I look back, I can see His hand of provision every step of the way.

Perhaps you've come to a point where you need God's provision. The weight upon your shoulders is too much. Although it may seem that no doors open, I am convinced that the Lord will provide answers. He will supply your needs. He will give you the resources and open the right doors. This chapter will provide you with sound biblical principles along with real-world testimonies that demonstrate that God provides for those who seek Him.

First, we will look at the different biblical references where people sought God's intervention and help. Second, we will examine four different areas where people need God's provision the most. Third, the final section offers hope when you find yourself in need, where your circumstances become difficult to negotiate. This chapter will encourage you and build your faith in times of adversity. As we begin, let's establish a biblical foundation in regard to the fourth prayer that God always answers: *the prayer for provision.*

I. Biblical Examples of God Answering the Prayer for Provision

The Bible refers to God's provision for those who seek it dozens of times in both the Old and the New Testaments. I've listed a few verses to help you see the way God responds to those who trust in Him:

Jacob prayed, "O God of my father Abraham, God of my father Isaac, O LORD, who said to me, 'Go back to your country and your relatives, and I will make you prosper,' I am unworthy of all the kindness and faithfulness you have shown your servant. I had only my staff when I crossed this Jordan, but now I have become two groups." (Genesis 32:9–10)

Follow my decrees and be careful to obey my laws, and you will live safely in the land. Then the land will yield its fruit, and you will eat your fill and live there in safety. You may ask, "What will we eat in the seventh year if we do not plant or harvest our crops?" I will send you such a blessing in the sixth year that the land will yield enough for three years. (Leviticus 25:18–21)

In everything that he undertook in the service of God's temple and in obedience to the law and the commands, he sought his God and worked wholeheartedly. And so he prospered. (2 Chronicles 31:21)

Because of your great compassion you did not abandon them in the desert. By day the pillar of cloud did not cease to guide them on their path, nor the pillar of fire by night to shine on the way they were to take. You gave your good Spirit to instruct them. You did not withhold your manna from their mouths, and you gave them water for their thirst. For forty years you sustained them in the desert; they lacked nothing, their clothes did not wear out nor did their feet become swollen. (Nehemiah 9:19–21)

"I know the plans I have for you," declares the LORD, "plans to prosper you and not to harm you, plans to give you hope and a future." (Jeremiah 29:11)

Give us today our daily bread. (Matthew 6:11)

I say to you: Ask and it will be given to you; seek and you will find; knock and the door will be opened to you. (Luke 11:9)

I will do whatever you ask in my name, so that the Son may bring glory to the Father. You may ask me for anything in my name, and I will do it. (John 14:13–14)

My God will meet all your needs according to his glorious riches in Christ Jesus. (Philippians 4:19)

These verses give us a broad picture of God's provision for those who seek Him. They cover basic necessities, finances, open doors, and the need for His presence. Three exceptional attitudes stand out in the prayers and circumstances mentioned above. First, these people expressed an attitude of thanksgiving for the past and for what they believed would come in the future. Second, they made a commitment to honor God and give Him the glory with the provision He gave them. Third, they expected His provision would come and, as a result, made preparations for its arrival.

Much like the prayer for freedom, I did not find a single Bible verse that mentioned God's refusal to answer someone's plea for His provision. I discovered incontestable evidence that God loves, helps, and takes care of those who put their trust in Him. As King David said, "Once I was young, and now I am old. Yet I have never seen the godly abandoned or their children begging for bread" (Ps. 37:25 NLT).

Throughout the remainder of this chapter, it's my goal to help you apply the central message of these Scripture verses to your life. What is that central message? You can count on God to supply your needs, open the necessary doors, and give you the resources you need. He will provide.

Do you feel fatigued because of a never-ending battle? Do you struggle with the sensation that you are not moving forward? If so, the following prayer will help you communicate with the Lord in a way that creates expectancy and builds faith. The prayer below is taken from different Bible passages where people just like you and me—people with the same types of needs and challenges—sought God's help, and He answered. If you need God's provision, reach out to Him with a sincere heart:

The Prayer for Provision

Lord, I give You my heart and ask for Your divine provision in my life. Give me eyes to see when You supply my needs. I give You thanks because I know Your answer is on the way. Throw open the floodgates of heaven and pour out Your blessing upon my life. I know that as I am faithful to follow, You will lead me; You will rebuke the devourer. I open my heart and thank You for Your provision in every area of my life. I will be faithful to administer every one of the things You entrust to me. In Christ's name I pray, amen.

This prayer is general, and you can use it to pray for your personal or family life. If you need His intervention in a specific area, I have outlined four areas where people need God's provision the most. The areas include basic needs, financial needs, the need for open doors, and the need for His presence. These are but a few of the areas where God provides for us.

These four areas will give you some powerful insights on how to recognize and welcome God's divine provision through prayer. We need only to have a genuine heart when we ask God to provide.

II. Four Areas Where You Can Expect Miracles

1. God's Provision for Your Basic Needs

In 1943, Abraham Maslow presented a paper on the psychological theory that broke down the five levels of human necessities. It's called the Hierarchy of Needs. He felt that some of the most basic human essentials were food, water, sleep, air, and homeostasis.[1]

No one understands these basic human needs more than the One who created us (Ps. 139:13). No one works harder than God to help us survive. Jesus tried to convey this to His followers when He told them that they didn't need to pour all of their emotional energy into worrying about the fundamentals of life (Matt. 6:34). He understands our circumstances and challenges, and He will provide all that is necessary for us to move forward (Luke 12:27–31). Jesus' message for us is simple: We need to trust Him before we allow ourselves to be consumed with anxiety.

In 1963, Richard Larson was teaching part-time at a private college. At the same time, he and his wife, Jan, were pastoring a small church in the Minneapolis area. They had a four-year-old daughter, a two-year-old son, and a newborn baby girl. The church of thirty-five people was too small to support the family. They struggled from week to week and paycheck to paycheck. Eventually, they found it difficult to buy the items families use each month such as baking supplies, starches, and oil.

One afternoon, Jan said to him, "Honey, we're out of food! There is nothing left to eat, and all of our sugar, flour, rice, and pasta is gone. To make matters worse, we have no money, and we are almost completely out of baby formula." It was a disheartening moment.

They sat down at the kitchen table, and he said to her, "Let's look through the cupboards and make a list of everything we need, including the items we'll need to replace in the next week or two. Then we'll pray over that list." As they went through the kitchen, Jan jotted down what her family of five would need in the days ahead. The list was long!

She put her pen down and placed the list in the middle of the kitchen table. They laid their hands on it and lifted up a prayer asking God to provide. "Lord, these are the things we need. We don't have enough money to buy the items that are on this list. We don't know where we can acquire these things without money, and we don't know what to do. But we believe that You love us, and we trust that You will provide for us."

Within five seconds of saying "Amen," there was a knock at the kitchen door. Larson got up to see who it was. The man standing on the step was notorious for his big smile that would light up any room. He was one of the church deacons where the Larsons were pastoring. He, his wife, and his son were holding grocery bags.

The man said, "Pastor, we just left the grocery store across the street. We were buying our groceries and thought, *We should pick up a few things for pastor. You never know what the Larsons could use.* So as we walked down the aisles, we threw in a few things here and there. Hopefully, you can use some of these items."

Larson stood in the doorway in shock and found it difficult to articulate his gratitude. He and Jan quickly placed the bags on the kitchen table and invited them in, but they said, "No thank you." Turning toward their vehicle, they said, "We have perishables in the car and need to hurry home. But we'll see you on Sunday." They never entered the house.

The Larsons stood on the outside step waving good-bye to the family that had so graciously blessed them. After the car left the driveway, Jan and Richard looked at each other for several seconds with dumbfounded smiles on their faces. Suddenly, the reality set in. They made a mad dash to the kitchen. Dumping the contents of the sacks on the table, they made a visual inventory of what the family had brought their way.

Richard looked at Jan and said, "Sweetheart, it seems to me that much of what we wrote down on that list is in these bags. Why don't we check the items on the list?" They checked off every item on the list. When all was said and done, there were two additional items the deacon had purchased for them that were not written down—one being a five-pound canned ham. The deacon and his wife had no idea the Larsons had a list—much less what was on it—but God did. And He provided more than what they asked.

When you feel anxious about the basic necessities of life, remember that God has the very hairs on your head numbered (Matt. 10:30). When you worry about food, water, clothing, or even air, remember that God provides nutrients in the soil and rain for the weeds that grow along the side of the road. How much more important are you than the wild shrubs that no one cares about? Besides, who can add "a single hour to his life" by worrying? (Matt. 6:27).

The prophet Elijah understood this concept very well. The great famine dried up the brook where he was living, and food was scarce. There wasn't any relief in sight. The Lord sent him to a town where a widow was gathering wood for her last meal. The Lord assured Elijah, "I have commanded a widow to feed you." When Elijah arrived by the main gate, he said to her, "Please bring me some water so I may have a drink." As she turned to find him some water, he added, "And while you're at it, can you bring me some bread, too?" She turned and humbly replied, "As the Lord is my witness, I don't have any bread. I have just a handful of flour and some oil. I'm gathering just enough wood to cook a meal for myself and my son before we die from this drought."

Elijah had compassion on her. "Don't be afraid," he said. "Go home and prepare your meal, but first, make a small cake of bread for me from what you have. Then bring it to me, and then make something for yourself and your son. For this is what the LORD, the God of Israel, says: 'The jar of flour will not be used up and the jug of oil will not run dry until the day the LORD gives rain on the land.'"

She returned home, mixed the ingredients, and made a

cake of bread for the prophet. She noticed that the flour did not run out nor did the oil run dry. Each day she was able to make enough food for Elijah, her family, and herself. God was true to His word. (Story paraphrased from 1 Kings 17:7–16 NIV.)

In a similar way, the Lord provided manna from heaven every day for nearly four decades for the Israelites who wandered in the desert. God never let them go a day without food.

If your current situation is discouraging and you seriously wonder if you will make it another day, ask the Lord for help. Ask Him to provide the basic things you need. He will bring together the necessary resources in order to see you through.

I encourage you to make a list of everything you need. Place your hands on the list and ask the Lord to open the doors, grant the resources, or provide the finances to meet each of your needs. Then ask Him to give you the ability to recognize His response when it comes.

The following prayer will help you find a starting point to articulate your basic needs to the Lord:

Lord, You know every one of my needs before I am aware of them. You see every challenge and every barrier. I ask You to provide all of my essential needs so that I can live and not simply survive. I know that You always provide more than what I need, and You never abandon me. Help me to see Your provision and to glorify You this day. I open my heart and express my gratitude to You for providing each one of my needs. In Christ's name I pray, amen.

2. God's Provision for Your Financial Needs

Have you ever been gripped with the fear that you might be living on the streets in the near future? One of the greatest anxieties we have today is the fear of running out of money. No one wants to be poor, and no one wants to be broke.

Our family lived in Central America for fifteen years. We traveled extensively throughout some of the poorest countries in the Western Hemisphere. We have seen good people struggle and even suffer. But God in His wonderful mercy constantly fights sin, corruption, and immorality to provide people with a better life. He works on every front to bring about solutions. Difficult financial times will come, but the Lord shows His mercy to those who trust in Him. It's worth noting that the prayer for provision should not be considered a proclamation of prosperity. Prosperity is surplus. Provision is meeting the need, and there is nothing in the Bible that suggests God hangs people out to dry. Even in the most desperate circumstances, God always has the last word, and He demonstrated that in Elisha's ministry.

The woman approached Elisha completely distraught. "My husband, your servant, died. You know he was a righteous man and how he loved the Lord with all his heart. The bill collector wants immediate payment for what we owe him, but I do not have the money. And now he is coming to take my two sons as slaves. Please help me!"

Elisha said to her, "Give me a list of all that you have in your house."

"I have nothing," she replied. "We are a family of little means. All we have is a little oil."

Then he said to her, "Go to each of your neighbors and ask them to give you all their empty jars, but don't underestimate what you can use. Take as many as they are willing to give you. Once you have collected a good amount, go back to your house, and shut the door behind you and your sons. Don't let anyone see you. Pour the oil from the jar you have into the jars that you and your sons collect from your neighbors. As each one fills to the top, put it in a safe place."

The woman and her sons went door-to-door asking their neighbors for any jars they were not using. Then, she took her sons and the jars they collected and shut the door behind them. As she poured the oil into the first jar, she noticed that the amount of oil from the original jar didn't diminish. "Quick, bring more jars!" The boys lined up the empty jars like an assembly line, and the widow kept pouring. When all the jars were full, she said to one of her sons, "Bring me another jar." "There are no more jars. We've used them all," he replied. At that moment, the oil stopped flowing.

She went to Elisha and told him everything that happened. He said, "Go and sell the oil to pay all your debts. Then you and your sons can live on what is left over." (Story paraphrased from 2 Kings 4:1–7 NIV.)

This is a powerful example of someone who had a financial need and did what she was told to do in order to prepare for God's answer to prayer. She collected enough jars so that her family could survive during the difficult times. Many times, people fail to prepare for God's provision, and, as a result, they struggle their entire lives. The widow, however, wisely did what the Lord instructed her to do.

In 1996, my dear friend Phil Guthrie received a phone call from a radio agent. The agent represented a woman who had received an AM station in Fresno as an inheritance, and she wanted to sell it. As the president of a network of stations, Phil was interested in acquiring it, but there was one major problem. "We're broke," he told the agent. "Well, don't let that stop you," the agent replied. "Why don't you come up to Fresno, meet with my client, and take a look at the station?" Phil kindly agreed to the meeting.

After prayer and a discussion about these things with a donor, Phil and his wife drove 225 miles north and had lunch with the heiress of the radio station. The installation sat on five acres of land and boasted a 3,000-square-foot office and studio. The station had the potential to reach half a million Hispanics. During the course of the conversation, Phil shared the vision of the network and then offered her a fraction of what she was asking for the station. He felt that if the Lord wanted the station to become part of the network, then He would work out the details.

The next day, the agent called and said, "I don't know what you said to my client, but she wants to sell it to you. She gave me instructions to move forward with the agreement: She will sell you the license for the station now and consider donating the land, the tower, and the building to your organization at a later date." Indeed, there was cause for celebration. However, even the fractional price was a significant financial hurdle to overcome—Phil wasn't kidding when he said the organization couldn't afford it. So he asked the Lord for direction, financial provision, and the ability to discern His direction. Soon afterward, he informed the donor he had previously prayed with.

The donor prayed again and felt that the Lord was guiding him to give to the project.

The day escrow was closing, Phil had to pick up the check from the donor, who lived about an hour from Phil's office, and deposit it into the escrow account before the end of the business day. Leaving in the afternoon, Phil rushed to complete the tasks on time. As he entered a portion of the freeway that was under construction, the long arm of the law pulled him over.

The officer wrote the ticket and added, "You *must* appear in court, because you were traveling too fast for this construction zone." The officer gave him the ticket and he continued on his way. Despite the obstacles, Phil was still able to pick up the check and make the deposit on time.

Weeks later, he appeared in court. He had wisely made a photocopy of the check and waited until his case number was called.

The first person to appear before the judge that day was a man caught fishing without a license. He was fined $800, and when he argued that he was unemployed, the judge slammed the gavel down and said, "You are ordered to pay $5 a week until it is paid!" After that verdict, Phil thought, *I'm toast.* His case was one of the last ones to be called that long court day.

Finally, the judge asked, "What are the charges?" "The defendant was traveling at eighty-three miles per hour in a construction zone where the posted speed limit is fifty-five miles per hour," the deputy responded. The judge looked at Phil and said, "What do you have to say for yourself?"

"Well, Your Honor, I run a nonprofit corporation here in the county, and I was hurrying to pick up and deposit a large check before the escrow deadline passed. We were completing the purchase of an asset for the corporation." "What constitutes 'large'?" the judge inquired. Phil responded, "Well, I gave your clerk a copy of the check." The judge abruptly responded, "That doesn't answer my question. What is 'large'?" "One hundred eighty-five thousand dollars," Phil responded. "That's really hard to believe." "No, Your Honor, it's true. Your clerk has a copy of the check." The judge motioned to the clerk and the clerk handed the check to the judge. The judge was shocked upon seeing the check that verified this unusual courtroom tale and said, "This is the best story I've heard all day! I can understand your circumstances, and I am going to be lenient with you, but you must go to traffic school. Good luck with your project. Next case!"

God not only met a financial need, but He opened a wonderful door to reach people every day with a message of hope. The next year, the owner donated the five acres of land with the tower and the building that contained the radio transmission equipment. Today, KEYQ 980 AM reaches hundreds of thousands of Hispanics in the Fresno area, and is one of thirty radio stations that carry my daily live radio program.

I don't think money is everything. However, I would rank it almost as high as oxygen on the list of human needs. Without it, it is very difficult to function in this modern age. And God knows it. If you need financial solutions because of debt, lack of employment, or other setbacks, place your faith in Him and lift up the prayer for provision. Ask the Lord to open the floodgates of heaven and provide the solution to the financial need you have.

I believe that once we decide to surrender our financial

dealings to the Lord, once we decide to genuinely move away from a life of debt, once we decide to be good stewards and people of integrity with what we have, God begins to bless us financially. He does so in many ways.

If you face financial challenges and need the Lord to provide a solution, I am sure the pressure you feel can seem overwhelming. I believe the Lord will provide the right solution. The prayer below will serve as a way to help you discover God's mighty hand of provision.

Lord, I know that You are sovereign and all-powerful. Everything is under Your command. If I have found favor in Your eyes, please provide for this financial need that I carry. Lift the burden that keeps me awake at night, and fill me with Your peace so that I no longer feel anxious about my temporary circumstances. I ask You to pour out a great financial provision during my hour of need. I commit to being a good steward with all that You've given me. Help me to walk away from the temptations that put me in this position so that I never have to live under this pressure again. I thank You for caring and providing. In Christ's name I pray, amen.

3. God's Provision for Open Doors and New Opportunities for Your Life

God's provision comes to us in many ways and manifests itself in different forms. Some people have tangible needs such as shelter, food, clothing, water, and basic security. Others have abstract needs that are more difficult to measure (esteem, love, and a sense of belonging). Some of us find ourselves at the brink of a major transition or in need of an open door. That's when we need God to provide clear direction for the new opportunity that could revolutionize our lives.

About AD 130 in the town of Sychar, a teenage girl was rummaging through some family heirlooms and came across the diary of her great-great-grandmother. The paper was withered, but the writing was beautiful. The diary highlighted one day when God opened an extraordinary door.

This is her great-great-grandmother's account of the day that changed the town forever:

Last Friday morning, I left the house with my empty water jar in hand and headed up to the well.

Along the way, I ran into Mirella, who said to me, "You're heading up early." "I'd like to avoid running into some of the other women," I replied. My friend just shook her head and smirked as I turned to head up the steady grade.

The well always had a certain appeal for single people. Many wonderful relationships started at the local drinking hole. Moses met Zipporah at a well. That's where Abraham's servant found Isaac's wife Rebekah, and, of course, we all know where Jacob met Rachel.

That day, it was especially hot. The air was completely still. Several hundred yards from reaching my destination, I noticed twelve Jewish men heading into town mumbling about the supplies they needed to purchase for their journey. The people of Sychar always said that I had a flirtatious personality. Personally, I have no idea what they were talking about.

But I must admit that as those twelve men passed me, I couldn't resist. I politely nodded and cracked a smile. But they didn't even acknowledge my presence.

I came to the well and stopped to catch my breath. That's when I noticed Him, a young man in His early thirties sitting alone in the shade. As I dropped my bucket to tie my hair back, the sound must have woken Him. He opened His eyes, paused for a moment and asked, "Will you give Me a drink?"

I thought that was peculiar. Jews normally never talk to us. Unlike the others, this man opened His mouth and said something. This piqued my interest, and I wondered if He wanted something else besides water. So I said to Him, "You are a Jew and I am a Samaritan woman. How can You ask me for a drink?"

He responded with something profound: "If you knew the gift of God, and who it is that asks you for a drink, you would have asked Him and He would have given you living water."

I didn't know His name. I had no clue who He was. I was certain of one thing. I came to the well that day to draw water—like I did every day, and He claimed to have something special He was willing to give me. A part of me couldn't tell if He was serious or teasing.

So I subtly asked Him, "Sir, You have nothing to draw with and the well is deep. Where can You get this living water? Are You greater than our father Jacob, who gave us the well and drank from it himself, as did also his sons and his flocks and herds?"

With that, He stood up and brushed off His clothes. Then He smiled and said, "Everyone who drinks this earthly water will be thirsty again, but whoever drinks the water I give him will never thirst. Indeed, the water I give him will become in him a spring of water welling up to eternal life."

I am embarrassed to admit that my internal reaction was not appropriate. I thought He was bragging about His wealth and could solve all of my earthly problems. I'd been to that well too many times, and I wasn't going there for just the water. I'd been in and out of relationships my whole life, and I wanted something that would last. So I exclaimed, "I want this water, so that I won't get thirsty and have to keep coming here day after day." I threw out the bait hoping he would take it.

One of the ways people find out if someone is involved in a relationship is to ask about their spouse. That's what I thought He was looking for when He said, "Go, call your husband and come back." I slightly smiled and said, "I'm not married."

All of a sudden, He took control of the conversation, and in a matter of five seconds, my life suddenly came to a standstill. To this day, I will never forget what He said to me: "You are right when you say you have no husband. The fact is, you have had five husbands, and the man you now have is not your husband. He hasn't even given you the dignity of calling you his wife. What you have just said is quite true."

Uh oh, I thought. *How did He find out about my dark past?*

I had misinterpreted the words of a holy man who I thought was interested in more than my ability to serve Him water. My past relationships had dirtied my mind and prevented me from seeing His true intentions. That's what happens when you've been involved with so many men.

I took a deep breath to regain my composure. I tried to avoid humiliation by sounding religious. "Sir," I responded, "I can see that You are a prophet. Our fathers worshipped on this mountain, but you Jews claim that the place where we must worship is in Jerusalem."

"Believe me, woman," He said with authority, "a time is coming and has now come when those who are faithful will engage in worship in spirit and truth. That's what God wants, people who are genuine and who desire His presence everywhere, anytime. It's who you are and the way you live that count before God."

For the first time in my life, I felt that I didn't have to have any masks on. He was the first man I had ever encountered with whom I could be transparent. In an attempt to find some common ground I said, "I know that Messiah" (called Christ) "is coming. When He comes, He will explain everything to us."

That's when He declared the most wonderful news I had ever heard: "I am He," He said. "You don't have to wait any longer or look any further." Jesus of Nazareth, the Messiah was standing before me.

Suddenly, His twelve associates came walking up the hill. They looked surprised to find us talking alone. Who could blame them? None of them, however, pulled Him aside and asked, "What does she want?" or "Why are you talking with her?"

I was overwhelmed with emotion. I had invested all of my energy in relationships that ended in bitter dispute. I had made mistakes too numerous to count. Yet at that moment, I met the one person who could redeem me and restore my dignity. He opened the greatest door of my life. It was a new opportunity that revolutionized my heart.

Without thinking, I dropped my bucket for the second time and sprinted back to the town with tears of joy streaming down my face. I ran so fast, I nearly fell twice. When I got to the town square just two blocks from there, I stood on top of the small wall surrounding the obelisk and shouted to anyone within the sound of my voice, "Come, see a man who told me everything I ever did. Could this be the Christ?"

At first, some of them believed me, and some of them didn't. But when they went to see Him face-to-face, they discovered that He was indeed the Savior of the world![2]

I love a great story, and this is how I imagined the Samaritan woman telling hers. It may be inconceivable for you to believe that she could have had a damaged view of the things Jesus was saying to her, but I can assure you that anyone who has been married five times has been around the block. The way they see the world cannot help but be affected by the past. As I mentioned in another chapter of this book, my stepfather was married five times before he met my mother. Regardless of my embellishment over some of the details of the story found in

John 4, the central point of the story remains unchanged. God provided her with an extraordinary new life at a time when she was struggling to survive day-to-day and from relationship to relationship. He was more than capable of working around her ill-conceived notions to bring salvation to her town—even putting His own reputation at risk.

How many times do we go to the same well looking for a solution to the same problems we face day after day, week after week, month after month, year after year? How often do we yearn for an open door or a new opportunity? I believe the God who provided an open door for the Samaritan woman on that special day that transformed her life is the same God who will open a new door and grant you a new opportunity. He is the God who provides open doors!

God knows what doors need to open in your life. He knows the transitions you face. He knows the new opportunities that must develop in order for you to move forward. He is not deaf. And He anticipates these things before you ever ask. He hears your prayers.

If you are looking for a new opportunity, like all prayer requests, I want to encourage you to write it down in a prayer journal. Make it a part of this prayer below and expect that He will open the door for you. Ask God each morning as you begin your day for open doors and new opportunities.

Lord, I believe that You are the God of open doors. I ask You to provide me with creative solutions, new beginnings, and limitless horizons. Fill me with Your presence and strength to walk through the door You are opening for me. Impart Your wisdom to discern which opportunity is the right one for me. I ask You to grant me favor and grace as I embark upon the new beginning You have for me. In Christ's name I pray, amen.

4. The Provision of God's Presence Even When You Can't Feel Him

Perhaps the greatest gift God can give us when our backs are against the wall is His presence. We may not be able to feel Him, see Him, or have any tangible evidence that He is there. But faith is about believing, and nothing is more comforting than knowing (believing) that God is standing in the gap with us. When we choose to walk with God, we never have to be alone again. God will give you His presence when you need Him. He will not abandon you.

Moses stood before the Lord at a watershed moment. The Lord said, "Leave this place, you and the people you brought up out of Egypt, and go up to the land I promised on oath to Abraham, Isaac and Jacob. I will send an angel before you and drive out the people in that land. Go up to the land flowing with milk and honey. But I will not go with you, because you are a stiff-necked people and I might destroy you on the way."

Moses was utterly dispirited, as was the entire nation. Everything he fought for suddenly didn't seem to have the appeal it once had. One thing was more important to him than anything else.

Moses offered the Lord a genuine rebuttal: "You have been telling me, 'Lead these people,' but You have not let me know whom You will send with me. You have said, 'I know you by name and you have found favor with Me.' If You are pleased with me, teach me Your ways so I may know You and continue to find favor with You. Remember that this nation is Your people."

The Lord patiently listened to his heart and said, "My Presence will go with you, and I will give you rest." Then Moses added, "If Your Presence does not go with us, do not send us up from here. How will anyone know that You are pleased with me and with Your people unless You go with us? What else will distinguish me and Your people from all the other people on the face of the earth?"

Moses had a valid point. What else can distinguish good from evil, holiness from sinfulness, righteousness from unrighteousness, or justice from injustice? Only the presence of God. If the Lord isn't with us, what purpose do we have in life?

Filled with love and compassion, the Lord answered his petition: "I will do the very thing you have asked, because I am pleased with you and I know you by name." (Story paraphrased from Exodus 33:1–17 NIV.)

Moses' humble reply struck a chord with the Lord. He managed to convey something that few human beings ever do. God's presence was more important to him than all the riches, property, power, fame, and glory in the world. Without the Lord's presence, it wasn't worth entering into the Promised Land. He would have preferred to stay in the desert where God was. Not very many people value God's presence as much as Moses did. That is why God answered his prayer.

What was it about Moses' heart that brought about God's positive response? Most likely, it was his humility, sincerity, and genuineness. He truly loved the Lord and loved being around Him.

Do you need the presence of God in your life? Are you wandering around in a desert looking for some sort of oasis or stream to quench your thirst? Friend, only God's presence can satisfy the spiritual dehydration you feel.

Recently, I was asked to preach in two open-air campaigns in Cuba. When the missionary there invited me to come, I responded with an immediate yes. After landing in Havana, my Costa Rican team and I drove five hundred miles to the east. We arrived in a town called Holguín, which is situated about 120 miles west of Guantánamo Bay.

During the afternoon of our first event, heavy rains pounded the area for three solid hours. Due to the weather, I wasn't expecting more than 150 people. At 5:00 p.m., the local pastors escorted us to an open-air lot that was located on the outskirts of the town. We drove up to an old building. Going from an air-conditioned vehicle to 95 degrees and 95 percent humidity is hardly pleasant. Our shoes plopped down into six inches of mud, and we made the short trek behind the building to the large field, where *seven thousand* people were waiting for the meeting to begin.

Many of them had traveled more than four hours standing in the back of dump trucks in the pouring rain. Because the crowd was so large, there weren't enough restrooms to adequately serve the multitude. The crowd overwhelmed us, to say the least. The people pressed against the stage and overflowed onto the platform. It was the first time I had ever been in a service where the crowd sang louder than the singers' voices coming through the sound system.

After a four-hour service, where more than one thousand people gave their hearts to Christ and asked God to forgive their sins, I watched them climb into the trucks that brought them. For many of them, it was a long trip back to their homes.

Personally, I don't know many people (myself included) who would make such a sacrifice just to spend time in God's presence. Most of us complain when the air-conditioning is too high or when the music is too loud. So why would our Cuban friends make such a New Testament effort? Christian history there points to this simple fact: The Cuban church yearns for God's presence. They live what Moses said: "If Your Presence does not go with us, do not send us up from here."

Today, they are seeing the revival they've prayed for. God is with them, simply because they ask Him to be. For them, standing in the pouring rain in six inches of mud in the Lord's presence is better than air-conditioning any day. The result of their desire for the Lord's presence is sobering. In the last thirty years, the church there has grown from approximately ten thousand people to more than a million.

What is your spiritual life like at this moment? Do you feel spiritually dehydrated? Do you lack God's presence in your life? If so, all you have to do is ask Him to walk with you, and He will.

I believe that once we are willing to spend a few moments of our precious time with the Lord, He will bless us with His presence. This is one of the greatest provisions of all!

The following prayer will help you initiate a new start with God so that you can begin to sense His presence in your life. Of all the things that matter in life, having God's presence is one of the most important. I strongly encourage you to pray this prayer or one in your own words everyday.

Lord, forgive me for cluttering my life with events, commitments, and responsibilities. Help me to filter out the things that are not necessary so that I can walk with You. I do not want to walk without You. Fill me with Your Spirit, and enable me to sense Your presence. Allow me to hear Your voice, and speak to me in a way that I can understand. If Your presence does not go with me, do not allow me to move forward. Allow me to experience Your powerful revival and renew my spirit. I thank You for the wonderful gift You've given me. In Christ's name I pray, amen.

III. The Miracle of a Second Chance

You may feel that there is no end in sight. Perhaps you have done everything right, but nothing seems to go your way. If that is the case, God offers you His powerful hand of stability. He will not abandon you even if you have turned your back on Him.

Simon was a fisherman who had financial challenges. He had taxes to settle, mouths to feed, and a crew to pay. After fishing all night long, he and his team guided their boats to the water's edge and began the laborious task of washing their gear.

Jesus was teaching by the side of the lake, and a large crowd gathered around to listen. They pressed in, making it difficult for Him to address everyone. He decided to distance Himself and create enough room so that everyone could see and hear Him clearly. Looking for a quick solution, He saw Simon washing his nets. So He got into one of Simon's boats and asked him to push out a little from the shore. Simon agreed.

After Simon positioned the boat, Jesus sat down and began to teach the people. As soon as He finished, He said to Simon, "Head out into the deep waters and let down your nets for a catch." Simon was reluctant at first. Any fisherman knows that the best time to fish is between midnight and 7:00 a.m. The worst time is when the glistening rays of the sun shine into the waters. However, Simon wanted to show the Lord respect. "Master," he said, "we fished all night long and didn't catch a thing. But because You say so, we will try one more time."

As soon as they let their nets down, they caught such an overwhelming number of fish that their nets began to rip. So Peter called to the other boat to assist them. Having two boats together enabled them to spread the nets farther and distribute the weight. Even then, they filled both boats to the point where they began to sink.

When Simon saw the miracle that took place, he was confronted with a stark reality. He was familiar with the miracles that accompanied the Lord's ministry, and yet he felt guilty. That morning wasn't their first encounter. Previously, he had begun to follow Jesus (Mark 1:16–18; Matt. 4:18–20), but he had returned to his old profession perhaps because of financial pressures. After all, Peter had a family, a home, and a business. The miracle he witnessed that day brought on a profound realization of his halfhearted, foolish, and sinful nature.[3] Simon fell before the Lord and said,

"Go away from me, Lord; I am a sinful man!" The Lord had compassion on him, because He saw his genuine heart. He said to him, "Don't be afraid; from now on you will catch men." In one powerful moment, Peter was given a second chance. Christ forgave his sin, offered him a phenomenal future, and remedied his financial pressures. In a matter of minutes, Simon and his crew caught enough fish to meet all their obligations. They learned that if they obeyed and trusted their Master, He would provide for them and their families.[4] They pulled their boats onto the shore, sold the fish, left everything behind, and followed Christ. (Story paraphrased from Luke 5:1–11 NIV.)

Indeed, during times of adversity, God shows Himself to be faithful in every area of your life, even when you walk away from Him. God knows every need you have, every challenge you face, and every barrier you want to break. He is more than capable of helping you overcome. "God is able to make all grace abound to you, so that in all things at all times, having all that you need, you will abound in every good work" (2 Cor. 9:8).

Many times we work hard to get ahead, but the thing we struggle with most is trusting and obeying the Lord. I've been guilty of worrying about too many things that are beyond my control. Perhaps, like Simon, you start trusting the Lord but eventually fall back into old ways. Even if you turned your back on the Lord and said, "I'm going to do things my way," the story above teaches us that He is patient and willing to work through our inadequacies and shortcomings. Why? Because He loves us beyond measure, and you are not an exception.

Perhaps you're doing all the right things, but nothing seems to be going your way. *The fish are not biting.* Ask the

Lord for help. Allow Him to step into your boat and give you instructions. You'll be amazed at the results that will come as a result of obeying and trusting in Him.

How can I make the statement that God always answers the prayer for provision? Because He is a sovereign God who cares about the needs of those who seek Him. He cares about the lilies of the field, the weeds along the side of the road, and even the creatures that swim ten thousand feet below the surface of the ocean. Yet, none of them worry about the rain, nutrients, or temperature. Whenever you wonder if the Lord will provide for your needs, remember: "The LORD God is a sun and shield; the LORD bestows favor and honor; no good thing does he withhold from those whose walk is blameless" (Ps. 84:11). So when you ask God to provide for you, expect that He will! *He is your provider.*

As we look back over this chapter, we've discovered that when you feel that your back is to the wall and you can't seem to move forward, you can ask the Lord to provide for each need you have. Write your needs down and present them as a prayer to the Lord. He provides the basic needs of anyone who puts their trust in Him. "So do not worry, saying, 'What shall we eat?' or 'What shall we drink?' or 'What shall we wear?' For the pagans run after all these things, and your heavenly Father knows that you need them" (Matt. 6:31–32).

The Lord understands that money is a very important aspect of human life. All wealth is at His disposal (Ps. 50:10), and He takes care of those who place their trust in Him (Ps. 125:1–2). Whether you seek an open door or a new opportunity, the Lord will provide a way for you to move forward.

Finally, of all the things we need in life, God's presence is the most vital. God freely provides His presence (Luke 11:13), wisdom (James 1:5), love (John 3:16), protection (Ps. 5:11), and mercy (Deut. 4:31) to all who seek Him. He will answer your prayer for provision.

All the prayers for provision listed in this chapter can be summed up with this simple two-sentence prayer: *Lord, provide for my needs. Help me to trust You in all things and anticipate Your divine provision.*

CHAPTER FIVE

The Prayer for Healing

❧

The doors of the ER flew open as the medical team rushed the gurney into the operating room. No one knew exactly what had happened, but the evidence suggested that she'd had a stroke. One of the doctors stopped to brief her husband: "We will do what we can." Her husband just looked down and somberly nodded. "We should have more information after we operate." Then the doctor turned and continued toward the double doors.

Earlier that evening, Cristina was in the shower when suddenly she grabbed the side of her head. In a matter of seconds, she lost her equilibrium and collapsed. At first it was thought she had fainted, but it was soon evident that the situation was much more serious.

As the family followed the ambulance to the hospital, they had difficulty processing the developing tragedy. It was hard to imagine that something so awful could happen to someone fifty-two years of age with no previous health issues.

Hours passed, and finally the doctor emerged from the

operating room. The somber look on his face suggested that the news wasn't good. "We don't expect her to recover. Most likely, she will be a vegetable, that is, if she survives the next week." Upon hearing the doctor's words, her husband closed his eyes and exhaled. The others simply stared helplessly at the tile floor in the waiting area.

Miraculously, Cristina survived the week. Although the doctors saw very little progress in her condition, they felt it would be better if she spent her remaining days at home. The family made the arrangements and took the necessary medical supplies.

Several weeks passed, with Cristina drifting in and out of consciousness.

One day, someone came to the door with a flyer that read "There Is Hope in Jesus." A four-night evangelistic campaign was about to begin about half a mile from their house. When Cristina overheard the conversation, she opened her eyes and whispered to her youngest son, Andrey, "I want you to take me to the campaign." Andrey wasn't religious, but he loved his mother and wanted to make her happy. So he and his father made arrangements to take her to the event.

They brought her onto the soccer field and sat down in the last row next to the sound booth. Her head was shaved and covered with a scarf. Judging by her appearance, I could tell that she needed a miracle.

During the course of the service, a notorious gang member entered the crusade through the far gate and approached the back of the crowd just behind the sound booth. Underneath his leather jacket was a 22-caliber pistol, which he intended to use on me. One of the ushers spotted him pacing back and forth with his finger on the trigger. The usher then alerted some of the other members of our team. No one dared approach him, nor did they bring it to my attention.

At the end of the message, I asked if anyone wanted to begin a new life with Christ. The gang member left the gun underneath his jacket and lifted his hand high in the air. He felt an overwhelming conviction in his heart as tears rolled down his cheeks. I came off the platform to pray with those who came forward and the gang member. After we prayed, he whispered to me, "Of all the things I need, a new life is the one I want most." Then he asked me to forgive him for his evil intentions. I happened to glance up and notice that Cristina was still sitting in the back with her family. The distraction wasn't enough to make me forget about her.

I turned and walked up the stairs of the stage and said, "There is a woman sitting in the back. Would those who brought her please escort her to the front? I would like to pray with you before we conclude."

The family brought her forward. I met them at the base of the stage. I placed my left hand on her shoulder and prayed, "Father, I ask You to heal this woman from the ailment that has affected her body. Glorify Yourself and honor her faith that she places in You. In Christ's name I pray, amen."

She turned and hugged her son and began to walk back to her spot. This time, however, there was something noticeably different. She didn't need any assistance. With each step, she looked amazingly more stable. By the time the meeting concluded, she was able to walk the half-mile distance back to her home.

Within a day, she was functioning and completely normal, without any evidence of a stroke. Perhaps the greatest miracle that happened that night was the greater healing that took place in her family. Her husband had struggled with alcoholism for years. Her son Andrey was involved in drugs and gangs. Her other son had been shot in the heart and lungs after he became involved in dealing drugs. He survived but was in and out of jail for several years. The entire family was struggling and in emotional anguish. When they saw the miracle that took place in Cristina's body that night, they became believers.

Her husband decided to attend Alcoholics Anonymous meetings and made a commitment to follow Christ. Since that time, he has remained sober, and their marriage has become healthy. Her son Andrey decided to leave his life of delinquency and began a relationship with Christ. Three years later, he started working full-time for our ministry and traveled throughout Central America with our team. Cristina's other son was released from prison and is attending church with the rest of the family. Five out of their eight children started walking with the Lord. Each member of the family experienced something wonderful as a result of the miracle that had taken place. The Lord works to bring healing to the body, soul, and spirit.

Sooner or later, in some way or another, everyone needs God's intervention. Whether we face a physical, psychological, or spiritual challenge, something will come our way that cannot be remedied by advances in science, medicine, or therapy. Many times, doctors have no solution, nor do counselors have the tools to help people make a breakthrough. No matter the circumstance, we can always turn to the Author of life and seek His help.

I carry a strong conviction that God works on every front to bring humankind to a better place. He works in the altars of campaigns and in the science laboratories of pharmaceutical companies to bring healing to the human body. He gives wisdom to the therapist, anointing to the minister, and discernment to the paramedic. He enlightens the scientist, motivates the doctor, and inspires the counselor. He gives insights to all who work to help people experience psychological, spiritual, and physical healing. Why? Because He loves us unconditionally.

I will never suggest that God heals every person who prays for a physical miracle. If that were the case, I could have stopped taking my blood pressure and cholesterol medications when I was thirty-eight. But I do believe that God offers answers, solutions, remedies, and open doors to those who seek Him. I believe that healing is not just a physical phenomenon. It is spiritual, psychological, and interpersonal. God's healing touches every area of our lives.

So when I suggest that this is a prayer God always answers, I want you to understand that God as our Healer touches our entire being: spirit, soul, and body. Throughout the Bible, God always heals spiritual iniquities, because He is the only one who can. In most instances, He heals our emotional wounds and our physical ailments. In doing so, He may choose to use modern science or an instantaneous miracle.

Perhaps you are struggling with a physical ailment, and the doctors cannot find a solution. Maybe you are struggling with an old emotional wound, and every time you remember the occurrence, the pain overwhelms you. Maybe your conscience is seared and you've lost all spiritual sensitivity. This chapter will provide sound biblical principles along with real-world testimonies to demonstrate that God provides physical, psychological, and spiritual solutions to the ailments we face. First, we will look at the different biblical examples of people who asked God to heal them. Second, we will see how God's healing can profoundly impact three areas of your life. Third, the final section offers hope when there seems to be no solution in sight. As we begin, let's establish a biblical foundation in regard to the fifth prayer that God always answers: *the prayer for healing.*

I. Biblical Examples of God Answering the Prayer for Healing

Of the seven prayers listed in this book, the prayer for healing is the most prominent in Scripture. The Bible refers to God's healing of those who sought it more than seventy-five times in both the Old and the New Testaments. I've listed a few verses to help you see the way God responds to those who seek His healing and the security that comes as a result of placing our lives in His hands.

Abraham prayed to God, and God healed Abimelech, his wife and his slave girls so they could have children again. (Genesis 20:17)

Isaac prayed to the LORD on behalf of his wife, because she was barren. The LORD answered his prayer, and his wife Rebekah became pregnant. (Genesis 25:21)

He was pierced for our transgressions, he was crushed for our iniquities; the punishment that brought us peace was upon him, and by his wounds we are healed. (Isaiah 53:5)

A man with leprosy came and knelt before him and said, "Lord, if you are willing, you can make me clean." Jesus reached out his hand and touched the man. "I am willing," he said. "Be clean!" Immediately he was cured of his leprosy. (Matthew 8:2–3)

News about him spread all over Syria, and people brought to him all who were ill with various diseases, those suffering severe pain, the demon-possessed, those having seizures, and the paralyzed, and he healed them. (Matthew 4:24)

Jesus answered, "Woman, you have great faith! Your request is granted." And her daughter was healed from that very hour. (Matthew 15:28)

He took her by the hand and said to her, "*Talitha koum!*" (which means, "Little girl, I say to you, get up!"). Immediately the girl stood up and walked around (she was twelve years old). At this they were completely astonished. (Mark 5:41–42)

He took the blind man by the hand and led him outside the village. When he had spit on the man's eyes and put his hands on him, Jesus asked, "Do you see anything?" He looked up and said, "I see people; they look like trees walking around." Once more Jesus put his hands on the man's eyes. Then his eyes were opened, his sight was restored, and he saw everything clearly. (Mark 8:23–25)

"That you may know that the Son of Man has authority on earth to forgive sins..." He said to the paralyzed man, "I tell you, get up, take your mat and go home." Immediately he stood up in front of them, took what he had been lying on and went home praising God. (Luke 5:24–25)

As he was going into a village, ten men who had leprosy met him. They stood at a distance and called out in a loud voice, "Jesus, Master, have pity on us!" When he saw them, he said, "Go, show yourselves to the priests." And as they went, they were cleansed. (Luke 17:12–14)

Five important lessons stand out in the verses listed above. First, God healed people to glorify Himself. Second, God's healing power not only touched the physical body, it also had a psychological and spiritual impact as well. Third, at times, the Lord's response came immediately. Other times, His answer came through a process and over a period of time. Fourth, God healed people because He had a destiny for them to fulfill. The result of their healing gave them the time and ability to fulfill something they would otherwise not have been able to. Finally, those who sought God's healing were genuine and sincere in their petitions.

When we apply these principles to our lives, we can have the expectation that God will bring us solutions to the ailments we face to bring Glory to His name. We can expect God to restore us emotionally and spiritually in spite of the ailments that affect us. If we believe that God has placed a destiny for us to fulfill, He will give us the ability and the necessary time to complete it. We can rest assured that if our hearts are genuine and sincere, He will work on every front to bring us answers to the challenges we face.

Today across Christendom, there are different interpretations in regard to how God answers prayer and how divine healing is defined. Some might deny that God uses an operation or medicine to restore someone's life. They would give modern science the exclusive credit. Some might argue that God hardly heals people and rarely interacts with humanity. This couldn't be further from the truth. In the cases mentioned in the Bible, God answered prayer using every available means at His disposal. I have yet to discover a verse where He turned His back on those who genuinely placed their trust in Him.

If you need healing in your body, soul, or spirit, place your hand over the location on your body where you are sick. If your ailment is emotional or spiritual, place your hand over your heart. Then pray this prayer every day with the expectation that a breakthrough is coming. The following is a compilation of different requests from people in the Bible who asked for God's healing and restoration.

The Prayer for Healing

Lord, I submit my life and heart to Your will. I ask You to heal my body and remove the source of this sickness. Bring me comfort, and rejuvenate every one of my cells. Provide Your clear solution to the ailment that is affecting my body, soul, and spirit so that I can live life and not just survive it. Restore every area of my being, and help me to recognize when Your solution comes. I place my life in Your hands and reject the enemy's attack upon this temple of the Holy Spirit. In Christ's name I pray, amen.

This general prayer helps us ask God for any physical, emotional, or spiritual needs for healing. The following three areas deal with this topic with greater specificity in case there is a significant issue you may be facing. These areas include healing for the spirit, soul, and body.

II. How the Power of God Heals Your Spirit, Soul, and Body

1. Experiencing God's Healing for Your Spirit

For the purposes of this chapter, we will assume that humans are trichotomous, that is, we are made up of three parts; spirit, soul, and body. "The word of God is living and active. Sharper than any double-edged sword, it penetrates even to dividing soul and spirit, joints and marrow; it judges the thoughts and attitudes of the heart" (Heb. 4:12). The spirit consists of conscience, creativity, and intuition or spiritual sensitivity. The soul is that which is psychological. It includes emotions, intellect, and will. I will use the terms *psyche* and *soul* interchangeably. Our physical bodies consist of genetics, molecular structure, and chemical compounds. Because these three are intertwined, many times a spiritual sickness can affect the body and the soul.

Spiritual affliction is the destruction of our faith in God by the sinful patterns we willingly embrace. According to Romans 1:28–32, when people reject the knowledge and leadership of the Lord, they become "depraved" and begin "to do what ought not to be done" (v. 28). The values listed there describe the spiritual sickness that plagues people who refuse the lordship of God in their lives.

Saul is a perfect example of this. He was someone who pushed aside God's rule and, with time, he became completely deaf to the Lord's voice. An evil spirit robbed him of his peace. Eventually, not even David's harp playing was a suitable remedy. Sadly, he never realized that the Lord's presence had left him.

Inevitably, sinful patterns that people willingly embrace bring on the worst stage of spiritual affliction—unbelief. Hebrews 3:18–19 says, "To whom did God swear that they would never enter his rest if not to those who disobeyed? So we see that they were not able to enter, because of their unbelief." One of the greatest challenges we face in life isn't political or financial. It's not substance abuse or some sort of Internet addiction. It's not racism or social injustice. It's not even Satan himself. It's unbelief. That's precisely why people walk away from God. That's why we see fewer miracles across this land than we do in other countries. That's why revival rarely touches a local congregation. Unbelief is the sickness that directly impacts our spirits.

I do not share what some preachers would assert: that people become sick because of a lack of faith. John chapter 9 disproves that notion. Instead, I believe that the danger exists when sickness wears down our faith. It causes us to lose heart. It discourages us. Blessed are those who find hope in Christ in spite of their physical battles. But my heart goes out to those who cease to believe because the pain has worn them out.

One of the great tragedies that can occur as a result of

sickness, death, and other calamities is the same one that comes from success, fame, and prosperity. When our trust in God begins to dissipate due to tragedy or success, we move away from the One who created us. And yes, that is a tragedy that God wants us to avoid at all costs. That is why He is concerned with the strength and health of our spirits, the one true facet of our being that is connected to Him.

The Healing That Destroyed the Man's Faith in Christ

He lived by the side of the pool in hopes of receiving a miracle. Occasionally, an angel of the Lord would descend and stir the waters. The first person into the pool was cured of his sickness. Because the man was an invalid, it was nearly impossible to be the first one into the water. His biggest obstacle wasn't his paralysis. It was his mentality. For nearly four decades he lived with the condition. His sickness was now part of his identity.

Jesus was walking through the crowd and saw the hundreds upon hundreds of people lying around waiting for the movement in the water. When He learned that the man had been there for thirty-eight years, He asked him, "Do you want to get well?" Instead of answering the direct question with a "yes" or "no" answer, he offered Jesus an excuse. "Sir," the man replied, "I have no one to help me into the pool when the water is stirred. While I am trying to get in, someone else goes down ahead of me."

Jesus discerned that the man didn't have the capacity to recognize a miracle when he saw one. His faith wasn't in God. His faith in God had dwindled significantly. His faith rested entirely on whether or not there was a line at the pool. For that reason, Jesus didn't argue with him or try to encourage him. He simply said, "Get up! Pick up your mat and walk." Immediately, the man was cured, picked up his mat, and walked. That day was a Sabbath.

The paralytic hadn't left the area when the Jews caught up with him and said, "It is the Sabbath. The law forbids you to carry your mat." Unfortunately, the man's soul and spirit hadn't been healed. In spite of the miracle, he carried deep wounds from thirty-eight years of suffering. Instead of expressing gratitude, he blamed Jesus for breaking the Sabbath. He replied to the authorities, "The man who made me well said to me, 'Pick up your mat and walk.'"

The Jews asked him, "Who is this fellow who told you to do such a thing?" He had no idea, because Jesus had disappeared into the crowd.

Time passed and Jesus found the man at the temple. He approached him and said, "I see you are well again. You better get your spiritual life in order and stop sinning or something worse may happen to you." Instead of heeding Christ's warning, the man went straight to the Jews and explained that Jesus was the One who healed him. (Story paraphrased from John 5 NIV.)

Some might argue that this man had great faith. After all, he waited 38 years by the edge of the pool for his miracle. Right? I beg to differ. If he was such a great man of faith, why did he join forces with the Pharisees and initiate the conspiracy to have Jesus killed in the book of John? Why did Christ sternly warn him not to continue in his sinful ways (or something worse would happen) well after he received his miracle?[1] Instead, I believe that the miracle was God's attempt to heal his nonphysical wounds. Unfortunately, the man refused the most important healing of all, the healing of his spirit.

Those who have an afflicted spirit may seem to function in society, but deep down they are tormented and twisted. Pharaoh rejected God's will time and time again. Although he knew the right path, he consistently chose to go against the Lord with the contorted intention of destroying a nation. Hitler is another example. He was determined to exterminate an entire people group. His conscience was completely seared, and his spirit was greatly infected. Saul's spirit was filled with darkness. He pursued David, a godly man, across the entire country. After sending three groups of soldiers to capture him at Ramah, he finally went himself. Upon his arrival, he stripped down naked and began to prophesy in front of Samuel, David, and his soldiers.

So what is God's remedy for an afflicted spirit? Is it physical healing? In many instances, it is. Physical healing inspires faith in God. In other cases, however, physical healing has little effect on people. As we see in John 5, physical healing didn't ensure psychological or spiritual healing. The once paralyzed and bitter man became a physically healthy and bitter man. So how does God heal the spirit from the negative traits found in Romans 1:28–32? God's healing comes when we make a radical decision to turn away from our wicked agenda. It comes when we turn to God and do whatever it takes to follow Him. A heart that is genuinely repentant discovers the healing presence of the Creator of the universe. The one thing the paralytic, Pharaoh, Hitler, and Saul all had in common was an unrepentant heart. They never made a radical decision to follow God and do His will.

If your spirit is afflicted, you can experience divine healing that will impact every area of your life. Make an about-face and agree to do what the Lord leads you to do. This prayerful decision is one of the most important ones you can make in life, because it will set the record straight between you and God. A healthy, godly spirit promotes a healthy psyche and a healthy body.

The following prayer is one that many people in our crusades have offered to the Lord. If you are sincere in your desire to follow God's lead, He will heal the wounds of your spirit that have caused the spiritual turmoil you face. Feel free to pray this prayer as often as you wish or when you feel spiritually disconnected from God, and keep it as a reference for the future. Like with every prayer, I encourage you to put these prayers into your own words.

Lord, I have allowed my circumstances to affect my ability to choose between right and wrong. I do not want my conscience to be seared. I want to be righteous in Your sight. I yield my will and accept Yours from this moment forward. Help me to see Your direction and to follow through with Your agenda. I purposefully turn from the evil patterns I have embraced so that I can be clean before you. Heal my spiritual iniquities and bring healing to my spirit. I ask these things in Christ's name, amen.

2. Experiencing God's Healing for Your Soul

The second area where we need God's healing pertains to our emotions and the way we think. Sometimes we carry pain for years, even decades. Bitterness, envy, lack of forgiveness, and self-hatred are the poisons we drink hoping to cause damage in others. The only one who is affected, however, is the person who ingests the poisons. A sickness that afflicts the soul can have a drastic effect on the spirit and body as well, and it can become psychosomatic.

For example, a woman who discovers she has a genetic predisposition toward breast cancer may become fearful even though she doesn't show symptoms. Her fear can cause fatigue, exhaustion, and complications with blood pressure. It can also affect her relationships and her faith in God. The Bible refers to the heart (soul) as being deceitful and impossible to understand (Jer. 17:9). Our emotions, although genuine, can be misleading. They can cause us to lose faith and doubt whether God is truly with us. The following short story depicts a man who fell into depression because of his sickness.

King Hezekiah succeeded his father as king of Israel, and he ruled as an honest and upright man. Over time, he became ill and was at the point of death. The Lord sent the prophet Isaiah to him with a sobering message: "Make sure all your affairs are in order. You are going to die, and you will not recover."

The news was devastating. He turned his face to the wall and prayed. "Remember, O LORD, how I have walked before You faithfully and with wholehearted devotion and have done what is good in Your eyes." Then, with a broken heart, he rested his head against the wall and wept bitterly. His illness was affecting his soul and his spirit. Hezekiah needed a physical, psychological, and spiritual miracle.

The prophet hadn't left the premises when, suddenly, the word of the Lord came to him again: "Go back and tell Hezekiah, the leader of My people, that his life will not end."

Isaiah returned to the court of the king, who tried to compose himself. His eyes still filled with tears, his heart with anguish. The prophet opened his mouth and said,

"This is what the LORD, the God of your father David, says: 'I have heard your prayer and seen your tears; I will heal you. On the third day from now you will go up to the temple of the LORD. I will add fifteen years to your life. And I will deliver you and this city from the hand of the king of Assyria. I will defend this city for My sake and for the sake of My servant David.' "

The prophet then turned to the attendants and said, "Prepare a poultice of figs and bring it." After making the composition, they applied it to the boil, and Hezekiah miraculously recovered. The prophet's words, however, weren't enough to convince the king that everything was going to be fine. His physical healing wasn't enough evidence either. Hezekiah felt deeply hurt and still felt uncertain of whether or not the Lord was with him. Before he could emotionally accept the fact that God had healed him, he needed more assurance.

He asked the prophet, "What will be the sign that the LORD will heal me and that I will go up to the temple of the LORD on the third day from now?" Isaiah could have responded, "Can't you see that you've recovered? Why do you doubt the word of the Lord?" Instead, he answered with compassion, and he told Hezekiah to pick a sign of his choice: "This is the LORD's sign to you that the LORD will do what he has promised: Shall the shadow go forward on the sundial, or backward?" The king answered, "It is a simple matter for the shadow to go forward. So then, have it go backward." His choice seems symbolic. He wanted time to go backward because he still feared the future.

Then the prophet Isaiah called upon the Lord, and the Lord made the shadow go backward. The Lord's gesture brought healing to his soul, and God graciously extended

Hezekiah's life fifteen years as He had promised. (Story paraphrased from 2 Kings 20 NIV.)

As it relates to physical healing, this story is exceptional and shouldn't be considered the norm. However, it illustrates a deeper truth that is universal and one I wish to highlight. Hezekiah's sickness profoundly affected his emotional state and his faith. This concerned the Lord, and He made the extra effort to bring healing to those areas of Hezekiah's life. God is concerned with our emotions. He is concerned with our spirits. He will make every effort to bring healing to those areas of our lives.

How does God heal the soul? He strongly urges us to live lives of forgiveness (Acts 8:23; Heb. 12:15; Eph. 4:31–32; Matt. 6:14–15; 18:21–22; Luke 11:4; 17:3–4; Col. 3:13). As long as we refuse to release the pain, we stay connected to the people or circumstances that hurt us. We stay emotionally bound to the affliction of our souls.

Many people come to our crusades with pain in their lives. Over the course of three or four nights, they discover God's spiritual healing that comes through the forgiveness of sin, and they receive the powerful benefit of extending that forgiveness to others. It's not uncommon that when they decide to forgive themselves, their friends and loved ones, and even the Lord, the pain they've carried begins to disappear. They begin to live lives of freedom. We have seen on more than one occasion where these same individuals experienced physical healing as a result of their spiritual and psychological healing.

There is evidence of this in the New Testament: "Confess your sins to each other and pray for each other so that you may be healed. The prayer of a righteous man is powerful and effective" (James 5:16).

When our souls feel downtrodden, the Lord may not send a powerful prophet with good news in our darkest hour, but He will attempt to get a message to us. That message is, "I am here. I love you. I will walk with you during this difficult time."

If you find yourself facing an illness that has brought on depression or is dismantling your faith, open your heart to God. Allow Him to heal your soul and spirit. When you make peace with the Lord, the effects of the physical illness begin to lose their powerful grip over your life, and many times that's when you can experience physical healing too. So ask God to bring healing to your soul every day, and release all your bitterness toward others.

The following prayer has helped many people experience a breakthrough over the power that their affliction has caused in soul and spirit:

> Lord, if I have gained favor in Your eyes, touch every facet of my being. I want to be a righteous, faithful person who is free from the emotional poison of anger and indignation. Help me in my unbelief. I ask You to show me Your love. Help me to see that You are with me. I release the resentment and bitterness toward everyone who has hurt or offended me. Heal my soul and spirit and bring whatever physical remedies are necessary so that I can be completely restored in my body. In Christ's name I pray, amen.

3. Experiencing God's Healing for Your Body

Some physical afflictions come and go. Others stay with us a lifetime. Some people are genetically predisposed to physical problems. Others are easily affected by their environment. Some people simply walk by a pastry shop and put on five pounds. Others eat what they want, smoke what they wish, and drink for forty years with absolutely no adverse effects. (I agree. It's not fair.) And, unfortunately, *we all grow old*.

A physical miracle is that which reverses the effects of a cellular mutation, chemical imbalance, faulty genetic code, virus, infection, or bacteria. How does God heal us physically? It's worth mentioning again that He uses every means available including all advances in science. If God would use someone like Pharaoh, why wouldn't He use modern technology to fulfill His divine will? I never discount any door God opens for us. In reality, every door He opens for healing is divine.

In addition to using modern medicine to heal our bodies, He also touches us directly. This can occur when we pray, when someone else prays, or when God simply says, "Be healed" (Matt. 8:16; Luke 5:24–25). Whether we go to the doctor or fall on our knees, we need faith to believe that a remedy exists for us. The following illustration highlights the importance of believing that, indeed, God has a remedy for you.

When the woman heard about a man who had the power to heal any disease, she crawled through the crowd in His direction. She had lived with a dangerous condition of hemorrhaging for more than a decade. It's unclear if the physicians of her day experimented on her or not, but one thing was certain: she had spent everything she had in search of a cure, and every time she went to a doctor, instead of getting better, she grew worse.

She was facing another dilemma. According to the social

and religious norms of her day, every person she brushed up against became contaminated by her condition (Lev. 15:25–33). Any woman with a discharge of blood couldn't simply roam the streets at will. She was refused contact with others.

The crowd surrounding Him was much greater than she had anticipated. Hundreds of people were pressing in to touch the Healer. As she stood on the outer perimeter of the multitude, she took a deep breath and decided to reach her goal in a most unorthodox manner. She dropped to her hands and knees and like a dog negotiated her way through the screaming crowd. With each advance she made toward the center of the mass of people, though, she made more and more individuals unclean.

In her mind, talking or praying with Him wasn't necessary. Even touching His skin wasn't necessary. She thought, *All I have to do is touch His clothes, and I will be healed.* Her thinking may have reflected a quasi-magical notion, which was common at the time.[2]

She finally reached the center of the crowd and, with all of her strength, lunged forward to touch the hem of His garment. Suddenly a surge of supernatural power was released causing her bleeding to stop immediately. There was no doubt. God, in His gracious and generous love for a woman who had suffered greatly, instantly healed her.

At once Jesus stopped, turned to His disciples, and asked, "Who touched My clothes?" The disciples seemed a bit taken aback by His question. "You see this huge crowd pressing against you, and yet You ask, 'Who touched Me'?"

He knew that God's power went out from Him, but He didn't initiate it. Someone flipped the switch, and that person hadn't asked permission. Jesus kept looking around for the individual. Finally, the woman came to Him filled with fear and trembling and told Him the entire story.

He recognized that she had tried every available remedy to be freed from her suffering. He also recognized that she was slightly misled in her thinking. The Lord, nevertheless, decided to honor her faith.

Before He dismissed her, He set the record straight. Notice that he didn't say, "My clothes healed you." Nor did He say, "The power of the almighty God healed you"—although that is, in fact, what happened. His reply said it all: "Daughter, your faith has healed you. Go in peace and be freed from your suffering." (Story paraphrased from Mark 5:25–34 NIV.)

There are several important lessons we can learn from this story. First, many times God chooses to bless us in spite of our erroneous thinking or even our misguided theology. The power of God doesn't depend on whether our paradigm is perfectly aligned with His. It's hardly affected by methodology or rituals. And as Jesus pointed out to her, it doesn't reside in one's clothing or possessions. Instead, it is activated when we place our faith in Him.

He responds to our faith, not our physical touch. Many people think that something miraculous happens at a point of contact or because we do something physical. Those things are wonderful and even powerful gestures, but in and of themselves, they possess no power. The power of God is released when we put our trust in Him.

This woman's story illustrates that when we place our faith in God we are never wasting our time. It never crossed her mind to say, "God, if it's Your will, I'm sure You have the power to heal me." Instead, she believed that every step she made toward Christ brought her that much closer to her miracle, her door to freedom. Just remember, when you feel like saying, "God, if it's Your will, You have the power to touch my life," God already knows what His will is. He is waiting for you to voice yours and to take tangible steps toward Him.

We can learn another valuable lesson from this woman. The woman expected something extraordinary to occur. She not only believed that it would be possible to grab hold of His garment in spite of the overwhelming crowd, but as a result of her encounter with Christ, something wonderful was going to happen. Her expectations were high. She managed to put aside the memories of twelve years of disappointments and believe that some sort of contact with the Healer held the key for a new chapter in her life. It pains me to see so many people give up and stop praying for breakthroughs. The years of disappointment have clouded their faith and ability to anticipate the wonderful gifts God desires to bestow upon them.

What new chapter in your life do you long to begin? Do you carry a wonderful expectancy in your heart? Or do the disappointments and hurts of your past prevent you from seeing a bright and victorious future? Do you find yourself in the midst of a battle that you have yearned to end for years? I believe that your faith placed in God is one of the greatest things you can do to move beyond the issues that hold you back. Your faith in Christ activates the power of God in your life, and yes, you can experience healing in all three areas: body, soul, and spirit.

Friend, if you find yourself in a place where you need a physical miracle in your body, and to date there are no solutions, I want to encourage you. Facing our mortality is never easy. It can be a difficult burden. I want to agree with you in prayer that God will either heal you, provide the medical answers you need, or divinely order the circumstances that will transform your quality of life. May God be glorified so that you will be able to fulfill His purpose and destiny for your life. Through it all, may your spirit and soul be enriched.

The following prayer is biblical and one that I have prayed thousands of times for people in every crusade for many years. We have seen thousands of people healed as a result of placing their faith in Him. May these words help you connect with the Author of life who brings healing to those who put their trust in Him.

Lord, if there is anything sinful that separates us at this moment, please forgive me so I can be in good standing with You. I ask that You heal my body from every source of disease and defect. I recognize that You are all-powerful and control all the elements. I receive Your divine healing and intervention. I reject any diabolical plans the enemy has for my body. May my genetic code and molecular structure align itself with the will of God at this moment. May every virus, infection, and bacteria be stricken from this body in the powerful name of Jesus. I thank You because I know You provide answers and solutions. Help me to recognize Your answer when it comes. In Christ's name I pray, amen.

III. Finding Hope When There Is No End in Sight

God is interested in all facets of our lives. He constantly works to redeem humanity from a fallen state in order to reestablish our relationship with Him. In one sense, He manifests that effort in healing us spiritually, psychologically, and physically. When we become discouraged, He encourages us to seek His help through prayer: "Is any one of you in trouble? He should pray. Is anyone happy? Let him sing songs of praise. Is any one of you sick? He should call the elders of the church to pray over him and anoint him with oil in the name of the Lord. And the prayer offered in faith will make the sick person well; the Lord will raise him up. If he has sinned, he will be forgiven" (James 5:13–15).

When there is no end in sight, it's easy to lose heart. If you've come to that point, try to remember that God's timing and His agenda are different from ours. His divine plan encompasses a much broader picture than we could ever imagine. Somehow, however, He incorporates our lives into that plan, and the outcome—though the timing might not be as we wish—is always part of His perfect plan (Rom. 8:28). Of all the miracles in the New Testament, none of them illustrate this point as powerfully as the following.

The man welcomed the afternoon breeze that provided a needed break from the hot sun. His skin was bronzed due to the fact that each day, he sat at the entrance to the temple and begged the religious pedestrians for money. He was crippled from birth and over time, he became an icon at the gate called Beautiful.

About three in the afternoon, two men were ascending the stairs that led to the entrance. In his typical monotone voice, he uttered his usual phrase: "alms for the poor." It is uncertain what caught Peter's attention at that moment, but he clearly saw an opportunity to glorify God in the midst of the religious center of Israel.

"Look at us!" Peter exclaimed with John standing at his side. Thinking that they were going to give him something of material value, the man looked to them with anticipation. Without hesitating or blinking Peter said, "I do not have any silver or gold, but I have something of greater value, especially in your case. In the name of Jesus Christ of Nazareth, walk."

Then Peter did something daring. He reached down, took him by the right hand, and helped the man up. The miracle wasn't gradual. It was immediate. His legs, ankles, and feet instantly became strong. Springing to his feet, he began to walk for the first time in his life. His experience was so overwhelming that he couldn't wait to show off the divine miracle that had taken place in his body.

So he accompanied Peter and John into the temple courts, jumping, running, and praising God with all his might. Within minutes a crowd of people gathered around him. They asked each other, "Is this the same crippled man who had begged for years at the temple gate?" There was no question as to the legitimacy of the miracle. This man, who spent his entire life as an invalid, was healed by the power of God. (Story paraphrased from Acts 3:1–6 NIV.)

I began this story by mentioning that God has His own agenda when it comes to timing. How many times did Jesus walk by that gate in His life? How many times did He see that same man begging for money? How many times did He feel his pain? It's true. Jesus could have healed him years before, but for some reason, He chose not to. In His divine timing, He had other plans. Instead, He saw into the future when two disciples would walk into the temple one afternoon. He knew that one powerful miracle at the right moment in the right place on the right day would glorify God in ways that it wouldn't if He were the one to perform it.

In the same way, no one can pretend to know God's perfect timing or His reasoning. I would never presume to understand why God heals people when He does. But I do believe that faith pleases Him (Heb. 11:6). I couldn't prescribe a spiritual formula that activates the Lord's healing power. But I believe that He never turns His back on those who place their trust in Him (John 14:18).

If you are in the midst of a turbulent storm with no end in sight, God will give you spiritual and psychological peace that passes all understanding. Isaiah 9:6 refers to Him as the "Wonderful Counselor, Mighty God, Everlasting Father, Prince of Peace."

Finding Significance in the Midst of the Storm

When I was attending college, a friend and I were driving from my mom's house back to the campus. We were involved in a conversation when, suddenly, I lost my train of thought. My friend asked me to repeat myself twice. Then, all I could do was pull the vehicle over. Waves of panic came over me. I was convinced that I was losing my mind. I was nineteen years old.

After several minutes, the fear subsided, but something worse was planted in my soul, the fear of being afraid. I became fearful that the anxiety would return. Like a self-fulfilling prophecy, it did. That week, I went to see a Christian family therapist. I sat down once a week and prayerfully discussed my past hurts, disappointments, family dysfunction, and tragedies. The anxiety eventually disappeared, but I still had to deal with the emotional pain that I had ignored for years.

During the first six weeks, I couldn't understand why God didn't make it all go away. I searched for a quick fix, but there was none. After several months, however, I discovered that God's healing was slowly taking form in my soul. I journaled. I talked. I prayed. It wasn't immediate; rather, it was a process. Although it was an emotionally shaky time in my life, the Lord guided me out of that turbulent storm to a safe, stable, and secure place.

I learned a valuable lesson through that difficult time. God gives us peace in the midst of the storm. I learned to say, "I praise you because I am fearfully and wonderfully made; your works are wonderful, I know that full well" (Ps. 139:14).

You, my friend, are fearfully and wonderfully created. God loves you, and He will see you through the darkest times. Whether you struggle with the pain of a hangnail or stage four cancer, the God of the universe is on your side. If your spirit is wounded and a chasm separates you from God, or your soul is full of anxiety, make peace with Him and allow the Prince of Peace to transform this dark chapter in your life. He will guide you out of the turbulent storm to a safe, stable, and secure place.

How can I say that God heals those who seek Him? Healing isn't limited to our earthly bodies. He heals our souls and spirits as well. "He heals the brokenhearted and binds up their wounds" (Ps. 147:3). If you ever doubt that God really cares about your circumstance, remember Christ's mission statement: "The Spirit of the LORD is upon

Me, because He has anointed Me to preach the gospel to the poor; He has sent Me to heal the brokenhearted, to proclaim liberty to the captives and recovery of sight to the blind, to set at liberty those who are oppressed" (Luke 4:18 NKJV). So when you ask God to bring healing into your life, expect that He will! *He is your healer!*

In this chapter, we've discovered that God provides physical, psychological, and spiritual solutions to us as we place our trust in Him. Our healing may be instantaneous or it may be a process. It may come as a result of a divine touch or through the medication developed in a science lab. God works on every front and uses intercessors, ministers, doctors, therapists, and scientists to orchestrate His goodwill to improve our quality of life. Placing our faith in God is the greatest thing we can do for our health!

The prayers of healing listed in this chapter can be summed up with this simple two-sentence prayer: *Lord, heal me. Break this affliction in my life and set me free.*

CHAPTER SIX

The Prayer for Blessing

T he militia gained momentum in the surrounding provinces of the African country. Soon, tanks rolled into the capital and toppled the dictator's government. Within months the church was forced underground. Concentration camps were established in strategic locations to absorb anyone who refused to accept the new regime. Nonconformists were ostracized from society and taken from their families.

The soldiers came in the early hours of the morning to take him to one of the camps. Sam clutched his wife and kids in one final embrace. As the men led him to the truck, his children cried out for him. He felt fear and anguish in a way he'd never known. His only crime was being a pastor of a small congregation. For two long years, the totalitarian rule tried to *recondition* him along with other Christian ministers, vagabonds, and homosexuals.

Although he was never beaten or treated harshly, seeing his fellow countrymen punishing those who refused to behave in the desired manner was demoralizing to say the least. The treatment was inhuman, but he never complained.

Upon his release, his wife and children were anxiously waiting. Much like their embrace before his incarceration, they didn't want to let go. The reunion was joyous until his wife mentioned their son's challenges.

"Sammy has problems in school," his wife said. "What do you mean, 'problems'?" he asked. "The teacher made him stand in front of the entire class. She told the students that people like him are the reason why there is so much suffering in the world, because he believes in God." Up to that point, Sam had managed to deal with the persecution, but seeing his son suffer was almost more than he could bear.

He quietly continued to pastor a small group of believers. For several years, their church services were held in the basements of abandoned buildings. The congregants entered the premises two at a time over a period of several hours. There was no preaching, no singing, no announcements, and no Sunday school classes. For several hours, they prayed silently.

Sam and his wife believed that God would provide for their needs and one day, He would bless them and help them move forward. He looked at his wife and son and said, "I know that these are difficult times, but just imagine how difficult they are for people who don't know the Lord." Then he repeated Joshua's words from thousands of years before: "As for me and my household, we will serve the LORD" (Josh. 24:15). They prayed and asked God for His blessing and His favor.

A week later, a local official summoned him into his office. The four-story building was the headquarters of the agricultural department which controlled all the farms in the country. Sam arrived early and walked up the rickety stairway and down the half-lit hallway. Thirty-five minutes after the appointed time of the meeting, the official emerged and said, "Please, come in." Sam humbly nodded, went into the office and sat down. The official closed the door, sat down behind his desk and leaned back in his chair. Five long seconds passed.

Then the man opened his mouth, paused and said, "I know everything you have done, and I know where you spend your time. I also know that you believe in God and teach people about the Bible." Sam was silent. "I believe you are a man of integrity. I am giving you a job, and provided you do it well, you won't have to stop pastoring your church. Instead of meeting in that old abandoned building, you can meet in your home. You have my word that no one will bother you from now on. By the way, I would appreciate your prayers." In a matter of moments, Sam saw the fruit of his faith in God.

More than four decades had passed since that time. As we talked, his aging eyes filled with tears of gratitude. "God saved my life and protected me from danger. He saved my family. He has greatly blessed us beyond anything we could ever imagine. My children and grandchildren are all healthy. My family loves the Lord. We prayed for God's blessing, and He answered our prayer."

That afternoon, I discovered a new way of defining the term *blessed*. Many interpret blessing as money, popularity, good looks, or an extended vacation. I believe that such things come from above, but God's blessings are much greater.

They are the spiritual, material, emotional, family, and

relational benefits that come as a result of His favor and approval of our lives. To a large degree, His blessings come as a result of keeping His commandments.

If you desire to walk in the blessings of God, this chapter will teach you how to pray for God's backing and favor upon your life. With an attitude of integrity, humility, and sincerity, you will experience His blessings in many areas. First, we will glance at the different verses that describe God's blessing upon the lives of those who sought Him. Second, we will look at five areas where God's favor can powerfully enrich our lives. Finally, the third section will offer an encouraging word when we feel disappointed or defeated. Now let's establish a biblical foundation to the sixth prayer God always answers: *the prayer for blessing.*

I. Biblical Examples of God Answering the Prayer for Blessing

The Bible refers to God's favor and blessings hundreds of times in both the Old and the New Testaments. Some of the following verses describe how God blessed those who asked Him. Other verses declare God's blessings upon those who keep His commandments. These verses point to one overarching theme: God blesses those who sincerely put their trust in Him.

> God blessed Noah and his sons, saying to them, "Be fruitful and increase in number and fill the earth." (Genesis 9:1)

I will make you into a great nation and I will bless you; I will make your name great, and you will be a blessing. (Genesis 12:2)

The LORD has blessed my master abundantly, and he has become wealthy. He has given him sheep and cattle, silver and gold, menservants and maidservants, and camels and donkeys. (Genesis 24:35)

Isaac planted crops in that land and the same year reaped a hundredfold, because the LORD blessed him. (Genesis 26:12)

Worship the LORD your God, and his blessing will be on your food and water. I will take away sickness from among you. (Exodus 23:25)

I will look on you with favor and make you fruitful and increase your numbers, and I will keep my covenant with you. (Leviticus 26:9)

All these blessings will come upon you and accompany you if you obey the LORD your God: You will be blessed in the city and blessed in the country. The fruit of your womb will be blessed, and the crops of your land and the young of your livestock—the calves of your herds and the lambs of your flocks. Your basket and your kneading trough will be blessed. You will be blessed when you come in and blessed when you go out. (Deuteronomy 28:2–6)

The LORD will open the heavens, the storehouse of

his bounty, to send rain on your land in season and to bless all the work of your hands. You will lend to many nations but will borrow from none. (Deuteronomy 28:12)

The priests and the Levites stood to bless the people, and God heard them, for their prayer reached heaven, his holy dwelling place. (2 Chronicles 30:27)

The LORD will protect him and preserve his life; he will bless him in the land and not surrender him to the desire of his foes. (Psalm 41:2)

From the fullness of his grace we have all received one blessing after another. (John 1:16)

These verses show us that when people seek God's blessing, He answers favorably. There are certain benefits to having faith and obeying the Lord. Some of them include God's spiritual gifts such as power, protection, and anointing. Other evidences of His blessing may consist of having a family, having a fruitful life, and having a positive impact on others and the generations that follow. Some blessings may come to us in the form of material provision such as an increase in finances, career advancement, and the necessary gifts to fulfill His call on our lives. One of the greatest blessings God bestows on us is the encouragement He gives us during our times of need.

In the several thousand verses I researched in writing this chapter, I did not find a single instance where God refused to bless someone who humbly asked Him.

What conclusion can we draw from these Bible verses?

We can rest assured that when we purpose in our hearts to keep God's commandments, He will "open up heaven itself to [us] and pour out blessings beyond [our]wildest dreams" (Mal. 3:10 MESSAGE). When we seek God's favor, His blessings will follow us, and His backing will rest upon our lives.

Perhaps you're out of sync with God, and as a result, you are not living a fruitful life. If you're caught in survival mode, God wants you to live a life full of abundance, meaning, and significance. If you long to experience the blessings of God in their fullness, the following prayer is a combination of what many people in the Bible have asked God to do. I encourage you to pray this prayer or one in your own words every day. Then be prepared for the overwhelming blessing He will pour out upon your life.

The Prayer for Blessing

Lord, I want to find favor in Your eyes and be in good standing with You. If You see that my heart is clean, I ask You to bless me spiritually, physically, psychologically, financially, and relationally. Grant me unprecedented favor in every area of my life. Enlarge my territory and give me the wisdom to manage the wonderful blessings that You will bring my way. I will give you all the glory for the blessings You give me. In Christ's name I pray, amen.

In general terms, this prayer can apply to your personal life, career, and family. God will respond to your petition to live a blessed and meaningful life. If you need a specific breakthrough, the following section will be of great benefit to you. I have outlined five distinct areas that offer godly insights on the prayer for blessing. They include God's blessing for your family and children, your labor and productivity, your needs, your finances, and your divine purpose and calling.

II. Five Areas Where God's Blessings Can Profoundly Enrich Your Life

1. Experiencing God's Blessing upon Your Family and Children

When families fall into the damaging patterns of dysfunction, it can have devastating effects for three and four generations. When a father teaches his family that following God is a waste of time, his children grow up transmitting that value to their children. Or when a parent is physically abusive, his children are much more likely to become abusive as parents. Many times, the cycle of destruction repeats itself generation after generation. The blessings of God hardly come to such a family when it is caught in sinful patterns.

On the other hand, when a family decides to keep God's commandments, it inevitably breaks the vicious cycle that plagued previous generations, and it sets into motion the favor of God over their lives and generations that follow. "You shall not bow down to them or worship them; for I, the LORD your God, am a jealous God, punishing the children for the sin of the fathers to the third and fourth generation of those who hate me, but showing love to a thousand generations of those who love me and keep my commandments" (Exod. 20:5–6). Every family wants to break free from the destructive patterns that keep it in dysfunction. The following account highlights my desire as a teenager to experience God's blessings and victory in my family.

"The blessing of God comes from an authentic relationship with the Creator of the universe," she said. "If you want to live life and not just survive it, you need to walk with the Lord and let Him lead your life." Those were the words of my friend's mom who sensed God's love for me during a time when my family was in turmoil. I was staying the week with them while my mom was tying the knot with her longtime boyfriend in Reno, Nevada. It was his sixth trip down the aisle to say, "I do."

Several years before, Mom and I had moved to a mountain community where we tried to start our lives over. I was thirteen. My dad made the long drive to see me every other weekend, and her boyfriend made the commute on the weekends. Although I adapted well to new middle school, Mom struggled to make friends. Many nights, she drowned her loneliness in a bottle of wine. Dysfunction left its mark on our family, but God had other plans.

The night when I heard the words about walking with the Creator of the universe, something in me resonated. When my neighbors invited me to attend church with them, I accepted. That's when everything changed. A miracle sparked an internal revolution. At first, there was hardly any evidence of a transformation in my life, but over the months and years that followed, God's redemption profoundly impacted my life. His blessings mark my life in every way, especially in my family!

When God reaches just one person in a family, His power begins to reach past, present, and future generations. God's blessing upon my life has obviously impacted my children. His blessing upon their lives has affected my parents. My mom became a devout follower of Christ and has completely turned her life around. She has been sober for fifteen years. My father married someone who loves the Lord, and together they attend church each week.

Love, *stability*, *peace*, and *respect* are the adjectives that I can now use to describe my family. Before the Lord was a part of our lives, it was completely different. God's power stopped the craziness and brought blessing where there was once chaos. God has blessed our family, and He will bless yours as well!

The Only Man God Found Worthy to Bless

Imagine a world filled with wickedness, sexual immorality, and evil. The Lord was greatly disappointed in man's behavior and grieved that He had made him. So He said, "I will wipe mankind, whom I have created, from the face of the earth—men and animals, and creatures that move along the ground, and birds of the air." There was one man, however, who found favor in the eyes of the Lord. His name was Noah.

The Lord instructed him to make an ark with sufficient room for a pair of every living creature so that they could survive the Great Flood that would destroy all life. "You and your sons and your wife and your sons' wives will be safe," the Lord said. Noah did everything the Lord told him to do. Then the Flood swept life away from the face of the planet.

When the waters subsided, God said to Noah, "Come out of the ark, you and your wife and your sons and their wives. Bring out every kind of living creature that is with you so they can multiply on the earth and be fruitful and increase in number upon it."

Then the Lord blessed Noah and his sons, saying to them, "Be fruitful and increase in number and fill the earth. Everything that lives and moves will be food for you. Just as I gave you the green plants, I now give you everything." Then the Lord made a promise that impacted all humanity for every generation. "Never again will the waters become a flood to destroy all life. Whenever the rainbow appears in the clouds, I will see it and remember the everlasting covenant between myself and all living creatures of every kind on the earth." (Story paraphrased from Genesis 6–9 NIV.)

With God's help, Noah was able to lead his family out of wicked, godless surroundings to a place where the blessings of God would abound. Since the time when God established His covenant with Noah, there has never been a worldwide flood. Noah sought God's favor, and God blessed him and his family and used them to change the world forever. For more than four thousand years, hundreds of generations have received the blessings that God initiated with Noah's family. The evidence of that blessing is a multi-colored arching sign across the sky that we continue to see today.

Friend, if you are looking for God's blessing for your family, seek His favor. Push aside everything that would cause a chasm between God and you, and He will respond to your sincere request.

If you desire to break the destructive patterns that have

impacted your family, the Lord will demonstrate His power to break the cycle. He loves you, and He will keep His promise. Although you and your family may be passing through deep waters at this very moment, God will paint His rainbow across the sky of your life.

The following prayer is meant to help you break free from all that has plagued your family so that you can begin to walk in His blessings:

> Lord, I ask that You break every generational destructive pattern that has affected my family. Erase every evil tendency in my family that previous generations embraced so that your favor and blessing can be upon this generation and the many that follow. Bless my spouse, children, parents, and siblings with Your health, protection, provision, and guidance. Fill them with Your presence, and may their relationship with You blossom. In Christ's name I pray, amen.

2. Experiencing God's Blessing upon Your Work, Career, and Productivity

When people are diligent in their attempts to be productive, the Lord rewards their efforts (Prov. 12:11). He blesses those who work hard to provide for their families (Prov. 31:15, 31). This is true whether you work in a secular corporation, nonprofit organization, or serve in a local church (1 Cor. 15:58). To date, I have yet to see a hardworking individual starving in any country where I have served as a missionary.

There is a distinction between God's blessing *us* for our

efforts and blessing our *efforts*. If we are diligent and genuine, He blesses both.

I am quite positive that you have faced resistance in your quest to produce results in your line of work. Economies become soft. Bureaucracies slow things down. Cultures change the way societies function. However, you can be confident that if you are doing what is morally right and what God approves, He will stand with you regardless of the opposition. God calls you with a purpose, and He gives you the necessary talents to complete the task. Part of that purpose is the work you do, the career you choose, and the productivity that comes as a result of your efforts. He will not lead you down a path and abandon you. He will help you be fruitful (John 15:1–5).

God's Blessing Is Unstoppable

Cyrus, the king of Persia, made a proclamation and granted the Israelites permission to rebuild the temple in 538 BC. He sent Zerubbabel to lead the charge with forty-two thousand Jews. The king gave them all the articles belonging to the temple of the Lord, which Nebuchadnezzar had carried away from Jerusalem when he took them into captivity.

The people who settled in Jerusalem when the Jews were in exile heard that the Israelites were rebuilding the temple and set out to derail their efforts. They intimidated them, made false accusations, and managed to convince the king to shut down the construction. For five long years, the temple project was at a standstill.

Zerubbabel had another problem. In order to complete the task, he had to dig out a capstone (the final touch) from a mountain and somehow raise it to the highest point on the temple. He had no army, no money, no support, and no energy.

That's when the Lord sent the prophet Zechariah to encourage him with these words: "'Not by might nor by power, but by my Spirit,' says the LORD Almighty. What are you, O mighty mountain? Before Zerubbabel you will become level ground. Then he will bring out the capstone to shouts of 'God bless it! God bless it!' The hands of Zerubbabel have laid the foundation of this temple; his hands will also complete it" (Zech. 4:6–9).

Indeed, God blessed his efforts. Zerubbabel, the prophets, the priests, and the rest of the Israelites picked up their tools and started to work again. When King Darius came to power, the hostile neighboring governors went to Zerubbabel and his leadership and asked, "Who authorized you to rebuild this temple and restore this structure?" They told them everything. So when the governors sent their report to the king, he searched his archives and found the decree that King Cyrus of Babylon had issued sixteen years earlier.

Darius then declared, "Let the temple be rebuilt as a place to present sacrifices, and let its foundations be laid. The costs are to be paid by the royal treasury." Then he told the governors to stay away from the construction efforts. Finally, he said, "If anyone changes this edict, a beam is to be pulled from his house and he is to be lifted up and impaled on it." (Story paraphrased from Ezra 1–6 NIV.) Through the prophet Zechariah, God made a promise to those who worked hard to raise up the new temple. The Lord kept His word. He blessed Zerubbabel's efforts, and in 516 BC the second temple was completed. There is no opposition—not even a political one—that can stop God from blessing those He chooses.

Are you looking for God's blessing and favor upon your endeavors? Do you feel there is opposition to your career, occupation, or calling? If so, ask for God's backing in this area of your life. Ask Him to bless you so that you can produce fruit that makes a difference, fruit that lasts. I have researched the different passages where individuals have asked the Lord to bless their efforts. The following prayer is a summation of those verses:

> Lord, help me to see Your perfect will for my life. May everything I do bring glory to Your name. Bless my hands, mind, and words so that I can become someone who produces fruit that endures the test of time. I want the end result of my life's work to count for something godly and eternal. Help me to connect with Your call and purpose for my life, and may my life's goal be in harmony with Your plans. I reject every evil strategy the enemy uses to discourage me from doing Your will. I resist his intimidation and distractions. I know that You will reward me for my efforts and thank You for Your blessings and favor upon my life. In Christ's name I pray, amen.

3. Experiencing God's Blessing in Your Time of Need

God's sovereignty suggests that He anticipates our needs well before we have them. This is good news, because there are times when we come to a point in our journeys and need real answers and workable solutions. That's when we can count on Him to respond in a way that we wouldn't necessarily expect.

A few months ago my friend called and said, "A church in another state invited me to become their pastor. My family and I have prayed and decided to accept their invitation. I know this is short notice, but the church where we currently minister needs someone right away. Can you preach the next four Sundays until the board can find an interim pastor?" I agreed without hesitation.

After the first Sunday service, the board asked me to receive the tithes and offerings during my remaining Sunday services with them. I was glad to help.

A week later, I stood behind the pulpit and opened my Bible to Malachi 3:11. I read how if we are faithful with our giving to the Lord, He will rebuke the devourer. I then stopped and said, "Friends, I have been faithful with my tithes, because I need God's help. We own a car that has a quarter of a million miles on it. As you can see, I need the Lord to rebuke the devourer." Everyone laughed.

After the service, an elderly man came up to me. "Jason, do you really drive a vehicle with 250,000 miles on it?" he asked. "I sure do," I replied. "Well, I am going to pray that the Lord will bless you with another car, because that thing is on its last legs!" I said, "Seriously, the car is fine."

Four days later, I received a phone call from my dear friend Don Judkins, who invited us to a celebration of his fiftieth wedding anniversary the following weekend. He said, "Jason, I went out and bought Maxine a new car for our anniversary." "That's wonderful," I replied. "You can have her old vehicle if you want. It has a little over fifty thousand miles on it. How does that sound?" I said, "If it's free, it's for me! Thank you very much. I'll take it."

We drove up to the anniversary party and returned in a car that was like new (especially compared to our other vehicle). The following Sunday morning, I approached the man who told me he was going to pray for me. I said, "Well, the Lord answered your prayers, because there is a newer car in the parking lot this morning." His face lit up. "Are you serious?" he asked. "Go look for yourself!" When he saw the car, he was more excited than I was.

Several weeks later, our vehicle with 250,000 miles threw a rod, and the engine froze up completely. That day, the motor met its doom, but not before God provided.

Someone prayed. Someone gave. The Lord blessed us with the answer just in time. But it all started with prayer.

Is there any doubt in your heart that God will bless you with an answer when you ask Him? When you find yourself in the middle of one of life's intersections with a significant need, do you really believe God would leave you without any solutions? If so, perhaps it's time to ask yourself what you truly believe about the character of God. Is He a God of love? Is He a God of provision? Is He a God of mercy? Is He a God who cares about your needs? If you are a sincere person who looks to Him for help, He will provide answers and blessings that will see you through to the other side.

In a long lineage of kings mentioned in the Bible, one person stands out for two verses. It is uncertain whether or not his father was alive at the time of his birth. The absence of a father would explain the mother's sorrow and anguish, which is the name she gave the child. When he grew up, he prayed, "Oh, that you would bless me and enlarge my territory! Let your hand be with me, and keep me from harm so that I will be free from pain" (1 Chron. 4:10). And yes, God answered his prayer. His name was Jabez.

He overcame the pain of his youth and the disgrace of his brothers. He believed that God would bless him and enlarge his territory, and the Lord answered his prayer. He didn't let the pain of his youth contort his view of a good and loving God. Perhaps your past is filled with sorrow and frustration. In your moment of need, you can call out to the Lord. I want to challenge you to pray the following prayer with conviction for the next thirty days. I believe that in the coming days and weeks you will see some phenomenal breakthroughs in your life as a result of making this a daily habit.

Lord, You know my needs and You see my heart. I ask You to provide a solution to this important issue I am facing. Make Your answer and direction clear for me to understand. I open my heart to receive each and every blessing You want to send my way. Keep Your hand upon my life, and I commit to giving You the credit and the glory. In Christ's name I pray, amen.

4. Experiencing God's Blessing upon Your Finances

The upper, middle, and lower classes all have something in common: money problems. Rich people are constantly protecting their assets from taxes, lawsuits, misappropriations, and fraudulent schemes. The middle class struggle to make enough money so that one day they can retire without fear of being tossed out on the street. The poor just want to keep their heads above water. Finances have always and will always be one of the fierce issues we face. Why? Because we need money for just about anything we do.

Four Things to Keep in Mind When Praying for God's Financial Blessing

God is not blind to the economic difficulties we endure. He desires to help us in our time of need. So how can we gain God's favor upon our finances? I will touch on four things to keep in mind when we pray. One of the sure ways to obtain God's blessing upon our finances is to recognize that it's not our money. It's His. We simply administer it. (If you don't believe me, try taking it with you when you die.) What happens to our money when we cease to live? The person we assigned in our will takes over as administrator. The same is true regarding our houses. If we don't pay our property taxes, the government removes us from the premises. As a matter of fact, nothing money can buy is truly ours forever. We've obtained it on a long-term lease. Even the government that runs the country is temporary. They administer the land until a more powerful entity removes them. One thing is certain, though: God owns everything (Ps. 24:1).

Second, if the Lord has everything at His disposal, wouldn't it follow that He will bless us if we commit to being good stewards? Many people pray for the blessings of God, but unfortunately, very few commit to break away from their incompetent and poor administrative habits. Instead of squandering the blessings that God has already given us, we should prayerfully commit to administer those blessings in a better way. Christ challenged us to be good stewards with these words from the parable of the talents:

"Take the talent from him and give it to the one who has the ten talents. For everyone who has will be given more, and he will have an abundance. Whoever does not have, even what he has will be taken from him" (Matt. 25:28–29). Commit to being a good steward, and God will bless you with more.

Third, we need to remember that, in spite of our misguided feelings that suggest God doesn't care about our financial issues, He is truly concerned about every aspect of our lives. He's interested in everything from our light bill to our car and mortgage payments, from our children's college funds to our retirement. Whether He blesses us with a miraculous and instantaneous response, or provides additional income through work, the Lord will answer our prayers.

Fourth, if the Lord chooses to answer our financial needs by giving us additional work or by opening a door, we need to be willing to do our part. Sometimes, God's blessings come to us only after we begin to move in a specific direction or begin to work toward a specific end. James says, "As the body without the spirit is dead, so faith without deeds is dead" (James 2:26). Paul states it this way: "If you don't work, you don't eat" (2 Thess. 3:10 MESSAGE).

God's Financial Blessing Comes from Where You Least Expect It

In Exodus 30:13–16, the Lord instructed Moses to collect a fee from each Jewish male for the upkeep of the Tent of Meeting. Over the centuries, this evolved into a tax that the Romans imposed on those who wished to keep their Jewish religious identity. Each year, they had to pay two drachmas, the equivalent of $80US.[1]

One day, Jesus and His disciples went to a house in Capernaum. The collectors of the temple tax came to the door, and Peter went out to speak with them. Knowing that Jesus was a teacher, they expected that He would be the most likely candidate in the group to pay the two-drachma tax. But He did not go outside to address them. "Doesn't your teacher pay the temple tax?" they asked. "Of course, he does," Peter replied. There was only one problem. Neither Peter nor Jesus had the money to pay it.

When Peter went into the house, Jesus asked him, "What do you think, Simon? From whom do the kings of the earth collect duty and taxes—from their own sons or from others?" "From others," Peter replied. "That is true," Jesus said. "After all, what king imposes taxes on his children?"

Although the Lord disputed religious practices and theological points with the Pharisees, He did not feel this was an issue worth debating. In His mind, people should pay what they owe. He then said to Peter, "So that we may not offend them, go to the lake and throw out your line. Take the first fish you catch; open its mouth and you will find a four-drachma coin. Take it and give it to them for My tax and yours." (Story paraphrased from Matthew 17:24–27 NIV.) The Lord did not make the payment appear out of thin air. Instead, He sent Peter to practice his old profession, where he had to put forth an effort to redeem his financial miracle. This story illustrates that God is capable of taking care of those who walk with Him and the financial burdens they bear.

The same is true for you today. Whenever you feel that your financial burdens are too much or the demands you face are overwhelming, don't be afraid to ask the Lord to help you financially. I strongly want to encourage you to be transparent with the Lord about your needs and have the full confidence to ask Him to bless you with financial solutions. I believe that God will respond positively to your request. "The blessing of the LORD brings wealth, and he adds no trouble to it" (Prov. 10:22).

If you need God's financial blessing upon your life, the following prayer has helped many people find the stability of God's hand in the midst of financial turbulence:

Lord, if I have found favor in Your eyes, I ask that You provide a solution to my financial challenge. Open the floodgates of heaven and pour out Your blessing upon my life. Teach me to be a good steward and how to administer Your finances in a way that is efficient and pleasing to You. I ask You to trust me with greater financial resources so that I can bless others. Help me to move beyond this challenge and to recognize Your answer when it comes. In Christ's name I pray, amen.

5. Experiencing God's Blessing upon Your Divine Purpose and Calling

Your *golden thread* is what you were created to be, why you're here, and what you'll be remembered for. It's your God-given call and reason for being. It's the one thing that makes you completely unique. Have you discovered your golden thread? God will bless you with wonderful gifts so that you can fulfill your calling and purpose. "Praise be to the God and Father of our Lord Jesus Christ, who has blessed us in the heavenly realms with every spiritual blessing in Christ" (Eph. 1:3).

God wants us to live a spiritually fruitful life and have an eternal impact upon other people. Whether we need the gifts of the Spirit found in 1 Corinthians 12:1–11 (service, work, wisdom, knowledge, discerning of various spirits, speaking or interpreting tongues, prophecy, faith, working of miracles, and healing), the fruit of the Spirit described in Galatians 5:22–23 (love, joy, peace, patience, kindness, goodness, faithfulness, gentleness, and self-control), or other gifts found in Romans 12:6–8 (ministry, exhortation, giving, leading, and showing mercy), we can expect God to bless us with every necessary resource in order to fulfill our golden threads. Is there a spiritual asset that you lack? Ask God, and He will generously give you what you need without finding fault (James 1:5). The following short story illustrates that God will give you exactly what you need to fulfill His call and purpose for your life.

"What do you want? Ask, and I will give it to you!" Those were the words God spoke to Solomon when he became king. He could have asked for all the riches in the world. He could have asked to be the greatest ruler or conqueror the world had ever seen. He could have asked for honor and fame, but he didn't. Instead, he asked the Lord for the most powerful gift of all. He asked for wisdom.

This pleased the Lord. He recognized that Solomon could be trusted, so He said, "I will give you a wise and discerning heart, so that there will never have been anyone like you, nor will there ever be. Moreover, I will give you what you have not asked for—both riches and honor—so that in your lifetime you will have no equal among kings. And if you walk in my ways and obey my statutes and commands as David your father did, I will give you a long life." God was true to His word. He blessed Solomon in every area, but most important, He gave him the one spiritual gift he needed to fulfill his divine purpose and call. (Story paraphrased from 1 Kings 3 NIV.) God gives us the spiritual blessings we need in order to complete the lifelong tasks He calls us to.

What are you lacking in order to fulfill your golden thread? Do you lack wisdom, power, discernment, or discipline? Do you lack the fruit of the Spirit? All blessings come from God. "Every desirable and beneficial gift comes out of heaven. The gifts are rivers of light cascading down from the Father of Light. There is nothing deceitful in God, nothing two-faced, nothing fickle" (James 1:17 MESSAGE).

I encourage you to write out your golden thread and ask God—using the following prayer—to bless you with the necessary gifts in order to fulfill His divine purpose and calling on your life. The Lord will equip you with everything you need to complete the task.

Lord, I lay my life before You. Reveal Your will and divine purpose to me in a clear and unmistakable way. I open my heart and receive every good gift that You want to impart to me. Grant me Your wisdom in order to make godly choices. Anoint me with Your presence so that I can have an eternal impact on those You have placed in my life. I want to be a good steward with every gift You have given me. Help me bring glory to

Your name with everything I do. In Christ's name I pray, amen.

III. God's Blessing and Encouragement Will Come to You

There are moments when we feel disillusioned because our families, friendships, or relationships are not supportive. When we feel disappointed or alone we can reach out to God and trust that He will meet us right where we are. One of the great gifts He gives us when we feel down is hope and encouragement.

The man was born blind. Every day, he made his way to the same place along the side of the road and begged for money. The disciples saw him, turned to Jesus, and asked, "Rabbi, who sinned, this man or his parents, causing him to be born blind?" The Lord replied, "Neither. Instead of asking that question, perhaps you should ask, 'How can we bring glory to God and help this man?'"

Then Jesus bent down, swished His mouth accumulating a decent amount of saliva, and spit it on the ground. Then He took His fingers, mixed it until the consistency was right, and rubbed the mud on the man's eyes. Then He said, "Go, wash at the Pool of Siloam."

The man found his way to the pool, washed out his eyes, and opened them. Immediately, the optic nerves became stimulated and sent signals back to the brain for the first time. Colors, dimensions, and images were suddenly interpreted by the cerebral cortex. A whole new world appeared before the man's newly developed eyes.

He leaped out of the pool and headed down the street

with a whole new spring in his step. His neighbors looked at him and said, "There is something familiar about that man. Is he the one who sat by the side of the road and begged?" Some were sure of it. Others were not. "Yes, I am that man!" he enthusiastically assured them.

When they asked him how it happened, he told them everything. When they asked where Jesus was, he said that he didn't know. Somewhat perturbed, they led him directly to the Pharisees, because it was the Sabbath.

When the Pharisees saw him, they said, "Now tell us from the beginning. What happened?" He said, "Earlier today, a man named Jesus bent down in front of me, spit on the ground, smeared the mud in my eyes, and told me to wash in the Pool of Siloam. So I did, and now I see perfectly."

Some of them weren't happy. "This man they call Jesus can't be from God. He doesn't keep the Sabbath." But others said, "That's ridiculous. If He was a bad man, He wouldn't be able to do miraculous things like this." Then they turned to the blind man and asked, "What's your opinion of this man?" "He's a prophet," he replied.

His response angered some of the Pharisees, even to the point where they questioned if the whole thing was one big lie, a farce. "How do we know you were truly blind?" Then they called the man's parents to verify his story. They came and answered, "He is our son. He was born blind, but we have no idea how he can see. He's of legal age; you'll have to ask him what happened."

They called the man in for a second round of questioning. "Let's put an end to this once and for all. Give God glory today, and don't lie to us again. We know this man is an impostor." The man replied, "Listen, I have no idea what you're talking about. All I know is, I was blind, but now I see."

For a third time they asked, "What did He do to you? How did He open your eyes?" The man lost his patience with their lack of intelligence. "I've told you over and over and you haven't listened. Why do you want to hear it again? Do you want to become His disciples?"

With that, they exploded. "Who do you think you are? You're probably a disciple of this fellow, but we are disciples of Moses. We know that God spoke to Moses, but we have no idea where this man even comes from."

"This is amazing. Your unbelief is a bigger miracle than my healing," the man replied. "I can't believe that you don't see the truth. No one has ever opened the eyes of someone born blind—ever! If this man didn't come from God, He wouldn't be able to do anything like this."

They exclaimed, "You're nothing but dirt conceived in sin! How dare you take that tone with us!" Then they threw him out in the street. Indeed, he won the debate, but at that moment, he was completely alone. His friends and parents were gone. No one stood by his side. It was the first time in history that someone born blind was healed, and even in light of all the evidence, the religious leaders accused him of being the lowly product of sin and put him out of the synagogue.[2]

When Jesus heard what happened, He went to the man and asked, "Do you believe in the Son of Man?" The man replied, "I would if I recognized Him. Tell me, who is He, sir? I want to believe in Him." Jesus responded, "You're looking at Him." The man said, "Lord, I believe," and he worshipped Him. (Story paraphrased from John 9 MESSAGE and NIV.)

While there are many profound lessons I could mention here, there is one sentence I want to highlight in this wonderful story: *When Jesus heard what happened, He went to the man.* This simple and concise sentence sums up the character of God and His infinite love for us. The Lord of lords took the time to seek out a man who was abandoned by his friends, neglected by his parents, and thrown out of the synagogue. He went out of His way to find one person. God searches for us at our lowest point, and that is one of the greatest blessings we could ever receive.

He reached out to Adam and Eve when they fell. He sent an angel to Elijah when he wanted to die. He forgave Peter after he denied Him three times. When we feel disappointed or defeated, the Lord Himself takes the initiative to connect with us and encourage our hearts. "The LORD himself goes before you and will be with you; he will never leave you nor forsake you. Do not be afraid; do not be discouraged" (Deut. 31:8). "Have I not commanded you? Be strong and courageous. Do not be terrified; do not be discouraged, for the LORD your God will be with you wherever you go" (Josh. 1:9).

If you've come to one of those low points in your life, you're not reading this by chance. Whether you have been ostracized from your family or rejected by your friends, God is seeking you out. He knows everything that has happened to you. He wants to encourage you, bless you, and express His love to you. He wants to ask you, "Do you believe in the Son of Man?" He comes to you at this time of need in order to connect with you!

There are two more things I want to share with you before we conclude this chapter. First, regardless of your age, it's never too late to start walking in the blessings of God. Moses was eighty when he stood before Pharaoh. Noah was five hundred when he started to build the ark. Abraham was eighty-six when he had his first son.

Second, always remember that you are a child of destiny. God has placed His hand on your life, and you are not here by some random evolutionary chance. God wanted you here, and here you are. He wouldn't have put you here without a reason. His divine purpose for you is beyond amazing. He has great plans in store for you. He will bless you with gifts, open doors, and provide resources in order to see you through.

So how can I make the statement that God always responds to the prayer for blessing? Because God doesn't lie. He promises to bless all who call on His name. "There is no difference between Jew and Gentile—the same Lord is Lord of all and richly blesses all who call on him" (Rom. 10:12). "God can pour on the blessings in astonishing ways so that you're ready for anything and everything, more than just ready to do what needs to be done" (2 Cor. 9:8 MESSAGE). So when you ask God to bless you, expect that He will! *He is the One who blesses you.*

As we look back over this chapter, we've discovered the many ways that God blesses us. According to the Bible, His blessings range from having a family to living an abundant life. They may come to us in the form of a financial breakthrough or divine favor. God's blessings are all that He deems as good, beneficial, and beautiful.

Many times, God's blessings come when our families break with old sinful ways, and He touches our children, grandchildren, and the generations that follow (Gen. 12:2–3). The Lord blesses our careers and occupations as we put forth a diligent effort. He helps us be fruitful, blesses us financially, and helps us in our time of need. He gives us every necessary gift in order to fulfill our reason for being here, our *golden thread*. "May God be gracious to us and bless us and make his face shine upon us" (Ps. 67:1).

The prayers for blessing listed in this chapter can be summed up with this simple two-sentence prayer: *Lord, bless me. May Your grace and favor be upon my life in every area.*

CHAPTER SEVEN

The Prayer for Salvation

I landed in Havana with five other members of a team to speak at a ministers' conference in the capital city of Cuba. The last night of our trip, we were invited to speak in a house church located on the outskirts of the city. We walked out of the fifties-style hotel lobby and asked the bellhop to flag us down a taxi. The young man grabbed the whistle hanging around his neck and signaled to the line of taxis that the next one should approach without delay.

The gunmetal-gray Toyota minivan pulled up and out stepped a forty-year-old man dressed in a dark blue suit and matching blue tie. His shaved head made him look older than he was. He took one last drag before throwing down his cigarette as he opened the side door for us. "My name is Enrique," he said.

My friend Dan had the directions and relayed them to the driver from the passenger seat. The rest of us spread out among the spaces in the back. Four minutes into our journey, Dan began to ask him a few questions.

"So, are you married?" "I was married, but I am divorced." "Do you have any children?" "I have three kids, one in her early twenties. The other two are teenagers." "Did you say that you have a daughter in her early twenties?" "Yes, I got started a bit early." "Do you see your kids often?" "Actually, my ex-wife lives close to where we're headed. I see them about once a week."

Then Dan took on a more serious tone and said, "You know, our lives are the sum of all the decisions we've made up to this point. The Lord loves you and wants to help you put your life back together again. Would you like to experience a powerful change in your life?"

Enrique responded, "Yes, but I am not sure how I can change. My life is really complicated. I'm embarrassed to say that I am one of the biggest womanizers on this island. That's why my wife divorced me. As if that weren't enough, I drink, and I smoke three packs a day. I've tried to stop my crazy behavior, but I am not sure what it's going to take."

We were quickly approaching the house church, and I knew that Dan needed more time to finish his conversation with our driver. So I poked my head between the two of them and asked, "Why don't you join us at our speaking engagement? We'll need a ride back to the hotel at 10:00 p.m. If you stay, we'll pay the meter." He enthusiastically said, "You have a deal!"

After passing thirty Russian-built apartment buildings, we arrived at our destination. More than fifty people were gathered outside the entrance waiting for the event to begin. We walked into the pastor's kitchen, and Enrique followed us. As soon as he crossed the threshold, he stopped in his tracks, looked at his arms, and said, "Wow!" I asked him, "What seems to be the matter?" He said, "I think there is electricity in the air." "Why do you say that?" I asked. "Because every one of the hairs on my arms is standing straight up. There's something different about this place." I just smiled and said, "You'll be just fine. I promise, it's not electricity."

After a short introduction and exchange of handshakes, the pastor and his wife escorted us to the patio area of their house. The crowd continued to grow, until nearly one hundred people had squeezed into the premises.

The six of us stood up to share our unique experience of how God broke the patterns of destructive behavior and transformed our lives. Enrique sat on the edge of his seat and hung on every word.

I took about ten minutes to share my story. Just before I finished, I asked the question "How many of you come from a crazy family?" Nearly half the hands went up. Enrique raised both his hands. Then I asked, "How many of you want to break free from the things that hold you back and begin a new life with Christ?" Twenty people raised their hands. Enrique jumped to his feet and said, "I do! I want to start my life again."

Several of them asked if they could share their stories. I didn't see a reason to object. So one by one, they walked to the front, spoke into the microphone, and gave their testimonies. That's when Enrique raised his hand.

He said, "Everyone else has shared something. I have something to say." I extended my hand to him and said, "Come on up." He moved behind the mike stand and said the following: "I've never spoken into a microscope before." Everyone laughed. "What did I say?" he asked.

"Anyway, I just want you to know that I am the worst man on this island. I'm a womanizing, drinking, smoking, undisciplined middle-aged man with a huge hole in his heart. But something happened to me tonight. It started on the way to this house church. When I walked into the kitchen, I felt something I've never felt before. Then when I heard the stories of those God helped to overcome the difficulties they were facing, I could see that there was hope for me. God is the only One who can fill that hole in my heart."

He paused, took a deep breath, and said, "I have never gone thirty minutes without a cigarette. But I've been here for two hours, and I have absolutely no desire to smoke. The craving is gone." Everyone applauded.

We said good-bye to the Cuban pastor and his family and headed to the minivan. On the way back to the hotel, Enrique wiped the tears from his eyes as he expressed his heartfelt gratitude toward a God who would save him from his sins. He said, "I feel like I've been born again." Dan looked at him and said, "That's precisely what just happened."

Enrique is a classic example of someone who recognized that his behavior caused a large chasm between him and God. He also recognized that he hurt the ones he loved. He sincerely wanted to change and, most important, he wanted to make peace with God.

Maybe you have a huge hole in your heart. Perhaps the way you think and the things you've done have destroyed your relationships and created chaos in your life. If your behavior has caused a large chasm between you and God, this chapter will help you bridge that gap so you can begin a new life.

The next few pages will provide sound biblical principles along with real-world testimonies to demonstrate that God breathes vibrant spiritual life into our hearts when we seek

Him, regardless of our past. First, we will look at the different biblical examples of people who turned to God for salvation. Second, we will see how God's salvation dynamically impacts three areas of our lives. Third, we will look at two individuals who lost hope, but whose lives were miraculously turned around as a result of making peace with God. This chapter will serve as a powerful spiritual breakthrough in your life. As we begin, let's establish a biblical foundation in regard to the seventh prayer that God always answers: *the prayer for salvation.*

I. Biblical Examples of God Answering the Prayer for Salvation

What is salvation? It is redemption from a state of spiritual lostness. It's the deliverance from sin and its consequences through faith in Christ. The Bible refers to God's salvation for those who seek it hundreds of times in both the Old and the New Testaments. I've listed a few verses to help you see the way God views salvation and how He responds to those who seek His spiritual redemption.

> My soul finds rest in God alone; my salvation comes from him. He alone is my rock and my salvation; he is my fortress, I will never be shaken. (Psalm 62:1–2)

> I pray to you, O LORD, in the time of your favor; in your great love, O God, answer me with your sure salvation. (Psalm 69:13)

> The moth will eat them up like a garment; the worm

will devour them like wool. But my righteousness will last forever, my salvation through all generations. (Isaiah 51:8)

She will give birth to a son, and you are to give him the name Jesus, because he will save his people from their sins. (Matthew 1:21)

The Son of Man came to seek and to save what was lost. (Luke 19:10)

God did not send his Son into the world to condemn the world, but to save the world through him. (John 3:17)

Everyone who calls on the name of the Lord will be saved. (Acts 2:21)

Salvation is found in no one else, for there is no other name under heaven given to men by which we must be saved. (Acts 4:12)

I am not ashamed of this Good News about Christ. It is the power of God at work, saving everyone who believes—the Jew first and also the Gentile. (Romans 1:16 NLT)

Christ redeemed us from the curse of the law by becoming a curse for us, for it is written: "Cursed is everyone who is hung on a tree." He redeemed us in order that the blessing given to Abraham might come to the Gentiles through Christ Jesus, so that by faith we might receive the promise of the Spirit. (Galatians 3:13–14)

Here is a trustworthy saying that deserves full acceptance: Christ Jesus came into the world to save sinners—of whom I am the worst. (1 Timothy 1:15)

These verses point to a universal theme throughout the Old and the New Testaments. God gives salvation to those who wholeheartedly decide to turn away from their sinful patterns and follow Him. In the Old Testament, sacrifices paved the way for individuals to be saved from the physical and spiritual consequences of their sinful behavior. In the New Testament, salvation comes through a genuine relationship with the Savior. Sacrifices are no longer necessary because of what Jesus did on the cross. "He is the atoning sacrifice for our sins, and not only for ours but also for the sins of the whole world" (1 John 2:2). "By that will, we have been made holy through the sacrifice of the body of Jesus Christ once for all" (Heb. 10:10).

So then, what must we do in order to receive salvation? We must sincerely acknowledge that we need God, make a significant effort to stop our spiritually destructive behavior, and follow Him. Paul answers the question this way: "If you confess with your mouth, 'Jesus is Lord,' and believe in your heart that God raised him from the dead, you will be saved" (Rom. 10:9). Salvation isn't the result of a simple prayer that we liturgically mutter. It comes when we genuinely decide to make Him Lord.

Are you looking for a brand-new start? Do you long to discover the true meaning of life? If so, the following prayer will serve as a guide to begin a real relationship with God.

I believe that as you pray this prayer, the Lord will honor your heart and bless you with the greatest gift of all, the gift of salvation.

The Prayer for Salvation

Lord, I thank You for loving me. In spite of my short-comings, You choose to accept me as Your child. I ask You to forgive my sins. Please take hold of my heart and allow me to begin a new life with You today. I believe that You rose from the dead, and in doing so, You conquered sin and death. I ask You to be my Savior and Lord. Give me the strength and courage to follow You all the days of my life. In Christ's name I pray, amen.

This prayer is a guide to help anyone begin a relationship with God. Not everyone is in the same place in life, however. Some of us have a limited grasp on spiritual matters. Others feel lost and simply want to find their way. Still some are looking for answers to life's toughest questions. Finally, there are some who feel as if they live in survival mode and want to experience a new beginning. In the next section, I will deal with two major questions in regard to the topic of salvation. Then I will address three areas where salvation in Christ can radically transform your life. Regardless of where you might find yourself in your spiritual journey, I am confident that when you finish this chapter, the road to true salvation will be clear and the new life that God desires you to live can begin. Now let's answer the question that serves as one of the motives behind this chapter.

Saved from What?

"Whoa, dude, that's pretty deep," my friend said to me. It was one of the first conversations I'd ever had with someone about salvation. I had just begun my spiritual walk with the Lord, and most of my friends were high school partyers. Just thirty seconds earlier, I ran into my buddy, who was fairly stoned outside the arcade. "Hey, man, how's it going?" he asked.

"I just gave my heart to the Lord," I said.

"Why did you do that?" he slowly asked as he squinted his eyes.

"I wanted to get saved."

"Saved from what?"

"From hell on earth and hell in the afterlife," I said.

"Well, why in the world would you be worried about the afterlife? You're only fifteen," he said.

"As I see it, I'll be dead a lot longer than I'll be alive," I replied. At that moment, the marijuana seemed to keep him from grasping what I was saying.

"Saved from what?" is the question that many people ask when searching for answers about the afterlife. The answer is simple: Christ came so that we could have life and have it more abundantly. He came to save us from hell on earth and hell after death.

When I say that He came to save us from hell on earth, I am not implying that life becomes a bed of roses once we begin a relationship with Christ. That is not the case. In some ways, when we become His followers, life becomes more complicated. Our relationships become volatile. Our families begin to question our motives. So in what way does Christ save us from hell on earth? The worst hell we can face on earth comes from the consequences of our own sinful behavior, excluding, of course, the rare tragedies that come to us by chance. In essence, He saves us from ourselves and the foolish decisions we make that bring destruction upon our lives in the here and now. This is one of the reasons we should become *followers*. When the Lord guides us, we live better, because the decisions we make in accordance with His will are in our best interests.

He came also to save us from eternal torment. All of humanity lives in a fallen state, and God gives us a lifetime in order to reconcile our spiritual debts and accept His lordship. If we fail to take advantage of His redeeming gesture before crossing the finish line of life, we enter into a state of utter and complete madness where there is weeping and gnashing of teeth for all eternity (Matt. 13:42; 24:51). At that moment, we become completely separated from God, friends, and loved ones. There is no peace, no joy, and no rest. God values us so much that He sent His only Son to save us from such a place.

Some might ask, "If God is loving and all-powerful, then why doesn't He grant eternal life to everyone?" This is an excellent question that merits a complete chapter to answer. But let me briefly say that God values our freedom to choose and doesn't force His will upon us when we don't want it. Thus, salvation is ultimately in our hands, because we decide whether or not we will transfer lordship of our lives over to Christ. While it's true that no one comes to Christ "unless the Father has enabled him" (John 6:65), God respects our free will and grants us the freedom to make that choice.

What Must We Have in Order to Be Saved?

Perhaps you've never been to church, and the idea of join-
ing a religion doesn't necessarily appeal to you. Between
you and me, it doesn't appeal to me either. Religion doesn't
save people. God does. If you have little knowledge of spiritual matters and feel out of your element, you need only
one thing in order to take the first step to begin a new life
with God: *a sincere heart.*

Why is this quality a recurring theme found in every chapter of this book? A sincere heart demonstrates humility. It
signifies surrender. Nothing pleases the Lord more than when
we are genuine and transparent with Him (James 5:16). The
following story shows how God forgives those who make
mistakes yet whose heart is in the right place.

His short legs made him agile. He was quick on his feet
and quick with numbers. Zacchaeus was the chief tax collector in Jericho and had acquired a great deal of wealth,
undoubtedly because he extorted and overcharged the people who traveled between his town and Jerusalem. This was
a common practice, which was why the religious leaders de-
spised people of his profession.

He heard that Jesus was passing through. His curiosity
was aroused by Christ's reputation of spending time with
people whose morals were questionable. Because of his
stature, he struggled to see over the heads of those in
the crowd who tried to get a glimpse of Jesus. So he ran
ahead and did something drastic. He climbed a sycamore-
fig tree just to have a bird's-eye view of the One they called
the Messiah. He stood on one of the main branches and
wrapped one arm around the trunk.

When Jesus was nearly beneath the spot where Zacchaeus stood, He paused, looked up, and called him by name: "Zacchaeus, come down immediately. I must stay at your house today." The statement sent shock waves through the hearts of those who were present. "What did He just say? Is Jesus actually going into the house of someone who swindles his own people?"

Zacchaeus was ecstatic. He immediately jumped out of the tree, landed on his feet, and warmly welcomed Jesus into his home. As they went, though, the people continued to murmur.

When their time came to a conclusion, Zacchaeus stood up and made a heartfelt declaration to the Lord in front of all those present: "Look, Lord! Here and now I give half of my possessions to the poor, and if I have cheated anybody out of anything, I will pay back four times the amount."

Zacchaeus knew he made mistakes and took advantage of others. His encounter with the Lord that afternoon, however, revolutionized his heart and his actions.

Zacchaeus was born into the house of Abraham because he was a Jew. When he met Christ, he was born into the kingdom of God. What was the one thing Zacchaeus had that allowed him to experience God's redemption? It wasn't his money. It wasn't his agility. It was his heart. He had a sincere heart, and in spite of all his imperfections, bad reputation, and conniving, his heart led him to the Savior.

When Jesus heard his sincere confession, He reiterated His mission loud and clear: "This is the type of person for whom I have come to help: someone who is spiritually disconnected from God." (Story paraphrased from Luke 19 NIV.)

If you feel lost and unaccepted, but have a sincere curiosity to know who God is, you are a perfect candidate to meet the Savior. You couldn't be in a better place at this moment. Salvation will come to you if you have a heart like Zacchaeus's; if you sincerely want to be saved.

II. How Salvation in Christ Can Profoundly Impact Three Areas of Your Life

1. Salvation in Christ Can Help You Discover the Right Direction for Your Life

Jesus answered, "I am the way." (John 14:6)

The Bible explicitly says that we do not get to heaven by working hard or by participating in rigid rituals (Eph. 2:8–9). All that is necessary is the desire to walk under God's direction. However, there are two things we must *do*, and they help us demonstrate to the Lord our desire to experience salvation. We must follow Christ on the path He chooses, and we must repent of our destructive behavior (Mark 1:15).

In both ways, Zacchaeus did what was necessary. First, he made the decision to walk on God's path. Whether you're starting from scratch in your spiritual journey or regularly attend a church, mosque, temple, or synagogue, choosing Christ is the right way to salvation. Jesus said, "I am the Road, also the Truth, also the Life. No one gets to the Father apart from me" (John 14:6 MESSAGE).

The Right Path

A few years back, I was on a missions trip in the jungles that stretch across the border between Panama and Costa

Rica. We got up early and drove in a rundown minivan that took us down a desolate dirt road. About an hour into our excursion, we arrived at the river that separated the two countries. We climbed into two eighteen-foot canoes that measured about thirty inches in width and crossed the river. When we got out, we continued for several miles on foot.

The place was crawling with snakes, beetles, and monkeys. In the late afternoon, we came to a fork in the trail, and the guide looked a bit pensive. He lowered his machete and grabbed his chin with his other hand. I asked, "Are you lost?" He responded, "I never get lost." I then replied, "Yes, I am sure that's the case, but are you lost now?" He said, "Excuse me, but I never ever get lost. I am the way to your destination." He looked around for a moment, nodded his head, and said, "This way."

He led us up to what looked like a wall of plants and thick rain forest. Within two minutes, he managed to hack through the jungle's elaborate foliage to our destination: a preaching point made up of four welded posts and a metal roof. I am quite sure that had he not been there, we would have never found our way.

When Jesus says that He is the Way, He doesn't imply that He is one of the ways to get to heaven. He emphatically means that He is the *only* Way. Choosing Him is what we must do in order to find the right path. Perhaps you're headed in the wrong direction and feel the need to get on the right path. If you sincerely turn your focus to Him and ask for help, He will guide you in the right direction. He is *the Way* when you are lost.

The second thing Zacchaeus did was to recognize the error of his ways, and with profound conviction, he turned away from his wicked behavior. After his initial encounter with the Lord, a powerful transformation took place in his heart that changed his inward and outward behavior.[1]

Repentance

"Dad, I'm lost," she reluctantly admitted.

"Sweetheart, it's almost midnight!" he said to his nineteen-year-old daughter. "Do you know what city you're in?" he asked. She paused before saying, "I have no idea."

Earlier that morning, his daughter's employer had set up a booth in a food fair located in the parking lot of a shopping mall. She had never been to the city prior to that day. The event ended at 11:30 p.m., and twenty minutes later, the phone rang.

"Don't panic. I'll stay on the phone until you get home. What street are you on?"

"Orange." There were six cities in their county with that name. To make matters worse, he had traveled to another state on business, so a rescue attempt would be out of the question. His mental picture of the city was the only way he could help her.

"Tell me the name of the next street you pass," he calmly said.

"Umm, it says, 'Kentucky.'"

He paused for a moment and said, "Okay, the next street should be 'Main.' Is that correct?"

"Yes, it is," she answered, surprised. "How did you know?"

"I'm familiar with the area," he said. "Now I want you to make a right on the next street, which should be 'Penelope.'"

"No, Dad, that doesn't seem right to me!"

"Excuse me, sweetie, but which one of us is lost?"

"Um, I am?"

"That's correct. So make a right!"

"Yes, that's the street," she said.

"Two blocks down, hang a right on Victory, and you should be within two blocks of the university."

"You're right, Dad. Thanks for your patience!"

Although she was heading in the wrong direction, she had the sense to ask for directions and the humility to stop driving around in circles. Within a few minutes, she was pulling into the driveway of the university.

Life contains uncharted waters, and it's very easy to lose our way. Sometimes our paradigm insists that we must head in a certain direction, but in doing so, we head toward disaster. However, if we repent (turn from our destructive behavior) and listen to God's direction, He guides us toward a life of blessing, meaning, and significance.

Christ is the Way, the one true guide who can keep you on the right path. When you feel disoriented and completely lost, He says, "Don't worry. I'll stay with you until we reach our destination. Turn right up ahead. The next street is Victory."

2. Salvation in Christ Can Help You Find Answers

Jesus answered, "I am ... the truth." (John 14:6)

Of all the virtues, truth is one of the most important. Without it, we would live in utter chaos. Truth is our foundation for life, and the most important truth God wants us to embrace is simply this: Christ is the answer for our lives.

Unfortunately, many people are deeply misguided and live by unfounded beliefs that carry them toward disaster. They doubt the existence of God, the divinity of Christ, and the authority of God's laws.

Over the centuries, many religions and philosophies have led hundreds of millions of people to believe in half-truths about life and the afterlife. Some teach that the way to heaven is to kill nonbelievers. Others teach that pleasure is the only intrinsic good for the soul. Still there are some that insist that after death, there is nothing.

All the religious and philosophical leaders who started these movements have one thing in common: They're dead. Their tombs contain corpses. Christ's tomb, however, is empty. Why is that so important? He predicted that He would be killed by the authorities and He would rise from the dead three days later (John 2:18–22). Through the Resurrection, He powerfully demonstrated that He was who He said He was. He is the truth, and if we believe Him, He will lead us through the complicated maze of life into eternity with Him.

One man in the New Testament tried to silence this truth. His name was Saul. He was a leader among the religious authorities in Jerusalem in the first century. When Stephen, a devout follower, was stoned to death for his faith in the Lord, Saul gave his approval and guarded the clothes of the executioners. Saul was so adamant about destroying the lives of those who believed in Christ that he went from house to house, dragging off men and women and putting them in prison. His life's mission was to eradicate all Christians, that is, until one day when everything changed.

The high priest sent him on a tour throughout the region to incarcerate any follower. He had almost reached Damascus when something amazing took place. At noon, a bright light from heaven flashed around him. It was so powerful that it knocked him to the ground. He heard a voice say to him, "Saul, Saul, why do you persecute Me?" He immediately discerned that the voice was divine. "Who are You, Lord?" he asked.

"I am Jesus, whom you are persecuting," He replied. In one sentence, Saul's life turned upside down. The man who had dedicated his life to the destruction of Christianity suddenly found himself face-to-face with the sovereign Lord. Without a doubt he thought, *Oh no! Everything I thought was a lie is true.*

The very next sentence Saul heard wasn't a polite invitation. It was a mandate to become a follower. "Now get up and go into the city, and you will be told what you must do," Jesus said.

The men who were traveling with Saul were speechless. They heard what was said, but they didn't see anyone. Saul got up and opened his eyes, but he couldn't see anything. They had to lead him by the hand into the city. There he remained blind for three days and didn't eat or drink anything, until the Lord sent someone named Ananias to pray for his healing. (Story paraphrased from Acts 9:1–19 NIV.)

Saul had a choice, to accept or reject the truth. When confronted with the reality that Jesus was Lord, he put aside his own beliefs and chose to follow Him. Saul, who later became the apostle Paul, experienced one of the greatest paradigm shifts in Christian history. He went on to be one of the first missionaries in Christianity and wrote 25 percent of the New Testament.

Paul's testimony powerfully illustrates that God patiently extends to us His grace and mercy in spite of our stubbornness. It illustrates that no matter what we believe, sooner or later, the truth will always come to the forefront. You don't need to be perfect or have the perfect set of beliefs in order to be saved. Like Paul, all you need is to yield to the Lord, and He will guide you to the truth. That's the starting point and the most important step of all. If you are confused and searching for answers, ask Christ to open your eyes to the truth.

3. Salvation in Christ Can Help You Experience Life

Jesus answered, "I am ... the life." (John 14:6)

God wants us to have life and have it more abundantly (John 10:10). When we invite Him to assume the place of authority in our hearts, He rescues us from spiritual death and the end result is true life.

Jesus said, "Are you tired? Worn out? Burned out on religion? Come to me. Get away with me and you'll recover your life. I'll show you how to take a real rest. Walk with me and work with me—watch how I do it. Learn the unforced rhythms of grace. I won't lay anything heavy or ill-fitting on you. Keep company with me and you'll learn to live freely and lightly" (Matt. 11:28–30 MESSAGE).

Working hard can burn us out, and it won't propel us through the pearly gates. Adhering to rigid religious rituals won't get us there either. Man-made theology imposes such rules on people, but God doesn't. He looks for those who are interested in a real relationship with Him.

* * *

The event began at 8:00 p.m. After an hour of worship and special music, the host invited me to the platform and gave me a very warm and kind introduction. I spoke for forty minutes and gave an invitation for people to begin a relationship with Christ. Several hundred people came forward.

A man in his midfifties dressed in a dark blue suit and tie deliberately negotiated his way through the maze of people until he reached the steps to the stage. He motioned to me, so I came down off the platform to speak with him.

His gold bracelet, cologne, and cuff links didn't identify him with the lower class. I assumed he had come directly from his office. "How can I help you?" I asked. "I don't know what to do. I feel so overwhelmed." He was very fidgety and wrung his hands together as his eyes shifted around the room.

He said to me, "I was feeling very anxious as I was driving down the street. Then I saw the sign hanging on the outside of this building that says, 'Come and experience new life.' I know what I've done is wrong, but I just don't know where to turn." I said, "It's going to be fine. Now take a moment, and tell me what's going on."

He continued. "My wife has been living in depression for nearly twenty years. We've tried various medications, but nothing has worked. In the last five years our relationship has deteriorated significantly. I was sharing my struggles with someone whose husband is a manic-depressive. We felt a mutual attraction, and for the last six months we've been having an affair. A month ago, I broke off the relationship."

He went on to say, "When I was a little boy I was taught that people who do what I've done burn in hell. I haven't been to a church in thirty years, but I am afraid my life's over. When I saw the sign, I thought there might be an opportunity to start my life again."

I said, "There is someone I want you to meet." I led him about ten feet to my left and introduced him to the pastor and his wife who have helped thousands of people find new life in Christ. I introduced them and briefly explained his story. The three of them talked for nearly an hour.

After the service was over, the pastor and his wife took me out for dinner. As we drove out of the parking lot I said, "Wasn't that man's story interesting?"

The pastor's wife spoke up, "Yes, but there is one problem with his story."

"What's that?" I asked.

"The sign doesn't say, 'Come and experience new life.'"

"It doesn't?"

"No."

"What does it say?"

"It says, 'Jason Frenn—International Conference Speaker this Friday, Saturday, and Sunday.'" Sure enough, when we drove by the front of the building, there was nothing on the twelve-foot sign that said anything about experiencing a new life.

A man who felt full of shame and carried a set of condemning beliefs saw a message on a sign that wasn't there. As a result, he discovered a new life in Christ. In the months following that night, he managed to reestablish his broken relationship with his wife, who courageously chose to forgive her. Together they began attending the local church. Although life hasn't been easy, they discovered the power of salvation that has renewed their lives and given them hope.

If you feel lifeless and dead, your salvation will not come in a set of rigid laws or rules that overwhelm you with impossible standards. Only salvation in Christ will help you discover true life (Gal. 5:1). Regardless of the errors you've committed or how bleak your future may seem, the Lord will revolutionize your life in ways you never dreamed.

The following prayer will help you begin a new life with Christ today. I want to encourage you to find a solitary place, take a few moments, and lift up the following prayer to the Lord. I am fully confident that He will hear and answer this prayer. He is the way, the truth, and the life.

Lord, I have little energy and little hope. My prognosis for the future doesn't look promising. I recognize that I need a change, so I come to You now and unconditionally yield my life. Fill me with Your presence. Give me Your strength. I want to be born again. Forgive all my sins and mistakes, and I ask that Your Holy Spirit would empower me to live a meaningful and significant life that glorifies You. I ask these things in Christ's name, amen.

III. God Offers Everyone a Second Chance

Jesus looked sternly into the eyes of Peter and said, "I have prayed for you, because just like Satan tempted Job, he has set his sights on destroying you. I've prayed that your faith will not fail, but when you turn back, make sure that you strengthen your brothers." "Lord," Peter replied, "I am ready to go with you to prison and to death." Jesus emphatically said to him, "Peter, before the rooster crows today, you will deny three times that you know Me." Peter couldn't believe it.

After they finished eating, Jesus led them to the Mount of Olives and told them, "Pray that you will not fall into temptation." Then he continued for about seventy-five feet so that He could pray alone. Not an hour later, He returned and found them all asleep. "Get up," He said. "Didn't I say you should pray so that you will not fall into temptation?" At that moment, the authorities came and arrested Him, and the disciples dispersed.

They led him to the house of the high priest, and Peter followed at a distance. Some of the servants of the household kindled a fire in the middle of the courtyard and sat down to warm themselves. Peter sat down with them. Sometime between 2:00 a.m. and 3:00 a.m., a servant girl glanced across the setting and said, "Haven't I seen you before? You were with the prisoner." "Hey listen," Peter said, "I don't know Him." From a distance, a rooster sounded the first alarm that daybreak was a few hours away.

A little later someone else in the group saw him standing over by one of the columns and said, "You are one of the followers of the prisoner." "That is not true!" Peter replied. Without Peter noticing, the rooster sounded the second warning. About an hour later, Peter could see the Lord's back from where he was standing. Another member of those working with the high priest came up to him and said, "Certainly you are with that prisoner. I can tell, because you are Galilean." Peter replied, "I don't know what you're talking about. Now leave me alone!" Just as he was speaking, the rooster crowed for the third time. The Lord turned around and looked straight at Peter. Then he remembered the words the Lord had said to him: "Before the rooster crows today, you will disown Me three times." Peter fell to the lowest level. He failed the test of faith, and in his defeat, he lost hope. He went outside and wept bitterly. (Story paraphrased from Luke 22 NIV.)

After the Resurrection, Peter said to several of the disciples, "I'm going out to fish," and they said, "We'll go with you." They spent the entire night but caught nothing. They were just about to give up, when they heard a familiar voice coming from the shore: "Friends, have you caught any fish?" "No," they answered. "Throw your net on the right side of the boat and you will find some," the man told them.

When they did, the number of fish was so large that they were unable to lift it into the boat. "Wait a minute," one of the disciples said. "I know that voice. It's the Lord!" They towed the boat and the net full of fish back to shore. When they landed, they saw a fire of burning coals with fish on it. After encouraging them to eat, Jesus turned to Peter and said, "Let's take a walk."

Jesus knew how Peter felt and remembered the last conversation He'd had with him. He said, "Simon, son of John, do you love me more than these?" Peter solemnly answered, "Yes, Master, You know I love You." Jesus said, "Feed My lambs." He then asked a second time, "Do you love Me?" This time, Peter slightly frowned and carefully pronounced his words: "Yes, Master, You know I love You." Jesus said, "Shepherd My sheep."

He said it a third time: "Simon, son of John, do you love Me?" Peter vividly remembered his mistakes as a disciple: One time he got out of a boat, walked on water, and within seconds started to sink when he took his eyes off Jesus. Once Jesus rebuked him and referred to him as Satan. He fell asleep when the Lord specifically told him to stay awake and pray for just an hour. And, of course, he remembered denying his Master three times.

He wasn't sure why the Lord inquired three times, but Peter was clearly upset about the Lord's tenacity. He hung his head, searched for the right words, and said, "Master, You know everything there is to know. You must know that I love You." Jesus looked at him with approval in His eyes and said, "Feed My sheep."

Then He repeated the same words He spoke to Peter the first time they met along the shore of the Sea of Galilee: "Follow Me!" (Story paraphrased from John 21 NIV.)

Jesus gave Peter a second chance. Perhaps, it was the biggest *do over* in history. This time, his faith would endure the distance. In the days, weeks, months, and years that followed, Peter became a great and devout follower of Christ. Why? Because he made peace with God.

He had a relationship with God but fell away. He slipped backward spiritually and needed to reconcile his life with the Lord. If the Lord would extend His grace and forgiveness to Peter time after time, in spite of his arrogant confidence, why would we doubt that He would extend His salvation to us this day?

God loves us so much that He sent His one and only Son to pay a price with His precious blood. We are so valuable to Him that He offers us time and time again an opportunity of redemption. As we see in the life story of Peter, He is the God of second chances.

If your relationship with God is weak and you are not at peace with Him, the Lord wants to offer you a fresh start, a second chance. If you know that you have allowed the cares and concerns of this world to pollute, dilute, and distract you from a simple yet real commitment to God, consider this moment. It's not by chance that this book is in your hands and you're reading these pages. This is a holy opportunity that God has orchestrated since the foundation of the world for you to make peace with Him.

Before I conclude this section, I would like to share with you an experience that had a profound impact on me. Although I've mentioned this story in another book, it merits repeating here.

The first night of our Ipis Crusade was energetic. Our tent had a seating capacity of five thousand people, but that first night more than six thousand people were in attendance. Many were standing thirty feet beyond the borders of the tent just to have a chance to see what was happening inside.

Two minutes before the service began, one of the ushers escorted a man down one of the aisles on the left side. She found the only available spot for him three seats from the aisle. She extended her hand in the direction of the vacant metal folding chair. He lowered his head and passed in front of the two individuals who were patiently waiting for the event to begin. His hair was a mess. His clothes were worn out, and he hadn't shaved in a week. The dark circles under his eyes indicated that he had a hard time sleeping. All of these things added an additional ten years to his appearance.

Within several minutes, 115 decibels were flying out of our professional touring sound system as the band kicked off a forty-minute set of praise and worship music. People were clapping and singing. Some raised their hands. The emotionless man just sat in his chair. He didn't move the entire time. Toward the end of my message, I gave an invitation to those who wanted to begin a relationship with God or recover the relationship they once had. He, along with 550 others, raised his hand and rose to his feet. With their hands in the air, the group made their way to the front where we prayed together.

I concluded the altar call by asking those who came forward to follow my crusade coordinator into the adjacent tent that served as our counseling center. Everyone headed in that direction except the man with the dark circles under his eyes. He just stared at me.

I signaled to one of our team leaders to personally escort him to the other tent. I knew that something was wrong, but I was unaware of his personal conflicts. The usher led him to the counseling center.

The next night he was sitting in the same seat forty-five minutes before the service began. During the music, he never moved. But when I gave the invitation, he raised his hand and stood. Just like the night before, he came forward and wound up in the adjacent tent with the hundreds of others to talk with a counselor. This happened each night of the campaign.

Several weeks after the event, my crusade coordinator called and said, "I managed to secure an interview for the ministry archives. We are going to videotape in two weeks. Can you make it?" "Sure, I'll look forward to it," I replied.

Two weeks later, I walked into our video suite where my team was waiting for me. Sitting in front of a camera was the man who was emotionless during the first few nights of the previous campaign. When he saw me, he sprang up out of his chair and embraced me. He leaned back to have a good look, shook his head, and continued to smile. His joy was contagious. I couldn't help but smile along with everyone else.

My coordinator said, "Jason, I'm glad you're here. We're just about to get started. Everyone, please take a seat." Soon the camera was recording, and the man began to tell us his story:

Awhile back my wife left me for another man, except she didn't leave the kids. She took them and moved in with the guy. I didn't have the resources to fight her for custody, and my business was quickly deteriorating. Eventually, I lost it as well. For six months, I struggled, but there was no end in sight. I spent countless sleepless nights thinking about how I could fix my money problems and my family problems. That's when I entertained the thought of ending it all. I tried to combine prescription pills with liquor but to no avail.

Last Tuesday, I was headed to a bridge. I was convinced that it was the only way to silence the diabolical voices in my head telling me to commit suicide. As I was driving down the street, I saw your two big white tents and the sign outside that reads "*Hay Esperanza en Jesús*" (There is Hope in Jesus). When I saw those words, I pulled over to the side of the road. I turned off my car and prayed one sentence: "God, if You exist, please help me tonight." I wanted a second chance. I desperately needed a second chance.

I came in the back of the tent, and there was one seat available. Almost a thousand people were standing, but God arranged for me to have a seat. You gave the invitation to begin a new life with Christ. *Is this the second chance God is offering me?* I asked myself. Night after night, I came, and night after night, I talked with a counselor afterward. Finally, Thursday night I prayed and asked the Lord to take the reins of my life, and He saved me.

Since that moment, I have been suicidal-thought-free. I am learning to let go of the pain my ex-wife caused me, and I made the choice to forgive her.

Two days ago, I started my new job, and I just got word last week that I can see my kids as often as I want.

Salvation in Christ has given me a second chance.

He finished his testimony and detached his microphone from his shirt. Hearing his words made me realize that anyone who loses all hope can discover a new life in Christ. Anyone is a candidate to experience the wonderful and powerful gift of salvation.

Assurance of Salvation Even When We Don't Feel It

There are times when we all question the reality of salvation, the presence of God, and the authenticity of the supernatural. Feelings don't get us to heaven. Faith does. Faith is acting upon our convictions even though we may not feel it's worth the effort. If you ask the Lord to help you—even in your unbelief—He will! "Everyone who calls on the name of the Lord will be saved" (Rom. 10:13).

How can I make the statement that God always responds to the prayer for salvation? Because Christ's mission is to seek and save that which is lost (Luke 19:10). The Bible promises us that everyone who calls on the name of the Lord will be saved. No person throughout the Bible who genuinely displayed the desire to follow God was ever rejected. You, my friend, are not an exception. "God did not send his Son into the world to condemn the world, but to save the world through him" (John 3:17). Salvation is God's plan, purpose, and destiny for your life! When you ask God to save you, expect that He will! *He is your Savior.*

As we look back over this chapter, we've discovered God's infinite love for humanity. At the core of God's heart is the desire to reconcile every human being unto Himself. Anyone who genuinely seeks the wonderful gift of salvation— that God so generously offers us—can expect to receive it.

When Christ is Lord of our lives, He saves us from hell on earth and hell in the afterlife. All we need in order to receive His redemption is a sincere desire to follow Him. Salvation in Christ provides us with *the way* when we are lost, *the truth* when we are looking for life's answers, and *life* when we have nothing to live for. Finally, no matter how many times we've failed or fallen away, the Lord offers us another opportunity.

Friend, if you find it difficult to sense God's salvation for your life, I want to offer you one final prayer that I have lifted to the Lord when I felt the need to start all over again. If you need a fresh start because your relationship with God is weak; or if you long to start over but you don't know where to begin, I am fully confident that this prayer will serve you well. It has helped me at several crucial moments in my life.

Lord, I know I've made too many mistakes. I am not perfect. Forgive me for not making our relationship the highest priority. I have let distractions and temptations pull me away. I want to be at peace with You, and I want You to be proud of me. Will You grant me a fresh start? I ask You to forgive me, and I ask You to accept me as one of Your precious children. I rededicate my life to You and ask You to give me Your Spirit to overcome everything that holds me back! In Christ's name I pray, amen.

The prayers of salvation listed in this chapter can be summed up with this simple two-sentence prayer: *Lord, save me. I surrender my life to You and ask You to be my Lord.*

Conclusion

❧

It was a long road trip with more than thirty-five speaking engagements in twenty-eight cities in twenty-five days. I headed into the final weekend completely exhausted with six events to complete. After driving two hours to take my wife and girls to Los Angeles International Airport, I fought three hours of traffic to the biggest banquet on the tour. My only prayer was, "God, please help me not to mess things up."

I arrived an hour and fifteen minutes late and walked through the door as they were introducing me to speak. When the night was over they raised more money than any year prior. I climbed into my car and headed back to the hotel.

The next day, I drove to the farthest city on the tour, which was five hours north. I finished at 9:00 p.m. and had to drive five hours south to a town where I had three Sunday services the next morning. After checking into the hotel at 2:00 a.m., I said to the night attendant, "I am going to need several wake-up calls in the morning. Why don't we set the first one for 6:30 a.m. and every fifteen minutes after that." She looked at me like I was from another planet.

I remember the words I muttered to the Lord as I stepped into the elevator: "God, I need Your help to wake up in the morning."

I literally crawled into bed fully dressed. Knowing that I had to get up in four hours, not one bone in my body looked forward to the next day. I closed my eyes and fell asleep. In my mind, only sixty seconds had passed when suddenly I heard a shrieking siren blasting in my room and on every floor of the establishment. The fire alarm forced everyone to evacuate.

People dressed in their pajamas were quickly moving their way down the hallways into the stairwell and into the lobby. As people congregated around the front desk, the hotel manager humbly announced that it was a false alarm. I looked up at the clock on the wall. It was 6:25 a.m. One thing was for certain. God had answered my prayer!

Within two minutes of returning to my room, the phone rang. It was the attendant. "Good morning, Mr. Frenn. This is your wake-up call." I thought to myself, *You've got to be kidding*. I think God was laughing.

* * *

As a missionary, the question I'm asked more than any other is, "Why don't we see the miraculous things in North America that people experience in other countries?" This question merits a much longer discussion than what we have time for, so I will be brief and to the point.

In the countries where people experience miraculous breakthroughs, God is a very large piece in their very small and simple puzzle. In North America and Western Europe,

God has been unfortunately reduced to a very small piece in our very large and complex puzzle. The key to seeing miraculous breakthroughs is to make God a bigger piece of our lives. When that happens, we will inevitably begin to experience something powerful. The best place to start is prayer. Spending time with Him will bring about the greatest changes and breakthroughs you will ever experience.

Let me add that most if not all of my colleagues who labor in Latin America, Africa, and Asia would agree that God answers the prayers listed in this book. In their minds, there would be little doubt that there are spiritual laws and promises every human can count on. Only in Western civilization do we question, overanalyze, and make spiritual principles relative.

I discovered three things as I researched and wrote about these prayers. First, my faith, along with the thousands of Bible verses I researched, led me to believe that God always answers the prayers mentioned in the pages of this book. Beyond a doubt, my faith influences my conclusions. Second, another theme became crystal clear as I began to write: God loves you more than you are capable of comprehending, and He will move mountains to see you through.

Third, while faith is an essential ingredient that helps us connect with God, it is not the most important. I discovered that a heart that is sincere and genuine is what the Lord values most. When we are transparent with Him about our requests, we can be assured that He will hear us and consider the petitions of our hearts. It's our only prerequisite as we pray.

Before I typed one word, I interviewed more than one thousand people to find out what prayer requests were most common. There was a direct correlation between the prayers people wanted God to answer and the ones He always answers. These prayers are not listed in order of any particular spiritual significance. I wrote them starting with the easiest and ending with the most difficult.

The Prayer for Direction

Of all the prayers that God answers, this one was the simplest to address. God freely gives guidance and direction to all who seek it. Throughout the Old and the New Testaments, only one person asked the Lord for guidance but was refused, and that was King Saul. His unfaithful, disingenuous, and unrepentant heart drove a chasm between God and him. Aside from Saul, every other person who asked the Lord for guidance received it.

As you apply this prayer, you can trust that God will lead you in a number of areas. When you struggle with the question *What am I doing with my life?*, He shows you a clear path toward purpose, significance, and meaning. When you pray the prayer for direction, you can look for Him to provide answers regarding your relationships, finances, health matters, and family.

There are times when we come to a crossroad and need God's help to see the best course of action. When we are unsure what the next appropriate step is, we can turn to the Lord for help. God always wants to lead, because He always wants us to follow. He shows Himself faithful to guide us in every area of our lives.

If you need God's direction, the prayers listed in chapter 1 cover many areas where you may need God's help.

The Prayer for Forgiveness

In the thousands of verses that I researched for this chapter, I discovered that God extended His forgiveness to people time and time again. Manasseh was the only exception. His unrepentant heart brought on waves of foreign raiders against Israel, because he filled Jerusalem with innocent blood. For that reason, the Lord was not willing to forgive him. However, in every other case, God graciously forgave every person who repented.

When you sincerely desire to be at peace with God, and you are willing to be transparent about your shortcomings, God will stretch out His loving arms and embrace you. Your mistakes are never too great for the Lord to forgive. Whether you have been sexually promiscuous, failed as a parent or disrespected your parents, behaved immorally, embraced materialism, or turned your back on God, when you pray the prayer for forgiveness, the Lord looks at you with a heart of compassion. He wants to redeem and forgive every one of your transgressions.

God's greatest statement of love came when He sent His Son to atone for every sin ever committed. That is what allows me to make the statement that God always answers the prayer of forgiveness. He felt that your life was worth the price of sending His Son to the cross so that your spiritual debts would be settled. He considers you the apple of His eye.

Regardless of what you have done, the prayers listed in chapter 2 will help you connect with God so that you can experience the power of God's forgiveness.

The Prayer for Freedom

The Bible says that Christ liberates the oppressed and sets the captive free. He breaks the evil strongholds that the enemy places on our lives. When we are stuck, struggle with vices, or fall into temptation, we can call on the Lord to break the chains that keep us bound.

The Old Testament lists many stories of people who asked God for deliverance, and in every case, He answered their prayers. Everyone who came to Christ looking for spiritual freedom was released from demonic oppression.

Whether you feel tormented and cannot find peace or you've lost your will to take another step, when you ask the Lord to deliver you, He will demonstrate His power in your life and set you free.

All authority in heaven and on earth rests in His hands. There is no principality or power of the enemy that can keep you away from God's loving arms. Christ sets you free not only from the forces of the kingdom of darkness, but from addictions, fear and anxiety, and the power of sin. Every human being is a candidate to receive this wonderful gift, and you are not an exception to that spiritual promise.

The prayers listed in chapter 3 are a compilation from the Old and the New Testaments and will help you connect with the power of God that sets the captive free.

The Prayer for Provision

The prayer for provision is written from a biblical perspective that holds that God provides for the needs of those who call on His name. In my research, I did not find a single verse that suggested God denied the prayers of those who sought His provision. The evidence is overwhelming. God loves, helps, and takes care of those who put their trust in Him. King David summed this up well when he said, "Once I was young, and now I am old. Yet I have never seen the godly abandoned or their children begging for bread" (Ps. 37:25 NLT).

There are different areas where you can apply the prayer of provision and trust that God will answer. Whether you need God's provision for the basic necessities of life, financial challenges, or to open doors leading to new opportunities, God's hand moves when you place your faith in Him.

Remember that God is sovereign and cares deeply about your needs. When you feel that your back is to the wall, ask the Lord to provide for each need you have. If you have difficulty seeing any progress, write down each request and present it as a prayer. He is the God of provision who never abandons those who turn to Him for help.

The prayers listed in chapter 4 are taken from different prayers found throughout the Bible. I trust they will be a great encouragement to your life.

The Prayer for Healing

God healed people in both the Old and the New Testaments. Sometimes, His healing was instantaneous. Other times, it came through a process and over time. It wasn't limited to just the physical body. God's healing touched the spirit and soul as well.

Several other aspects stand out in regard to healing. First,

God heals people to glorify Himself. Second, the result of His healing gives people the time and ability to fulfill something they would otherwise not be able to. Finally, God is pleased when people ask Him for His miraculous touch when they wholeheartedly put their faith in Him.

Whether we face a spiritual, psychological, or physical infirmity, God uses every resource available to bring healing to our lives. He can use a pharmaceutical breakthrough, a counselor, a minister, or a doctor to orchestrate the solutions we need. He is not limited by our paradigms, theology, or expectations that force Him into a box.

God is always willing to heal our spiritual iniquities, mostly because He is the only One who can. In most instances, He heals our emotional wounds, and sometimes, He heals our bodies by divine touch.

Regardless if you go to the doctor or fall on your knees, you need faith to believe that a remedy exists for you and that God has everything under control. Your faith placed in God is one of the greatest things you can do to move beyond the issues that hold you back.

The prayers listed throughout chapter 5 will help you pray and discover God's physical, psychological, and spiritual healing.

The Prayer for Blessing

Although many people define the word *blessing* in terms of finances, having good looks, or receiving an extended paid vacation with a complimentary spa treatment, God's blessings are much greater. They encompass spiritual, material, emotional, family, and relational benefits as well.

They come as a result of God's favor and approval of our lives.

According to the Bible, there are many areas where God blesses us. I have listed the five most recurring. They are: His blessing upon our families (spouse, children, and the generations that follow), our work (career and productivity), our needs, and our finances. Finally, He gives us the necessary gifts to carry out His divine purpose and calling upon our lives.

Perhaps the greatest blessings God bestows upon our lives are His presence and His infinite love for us. The God of the universe takes time to find us at our lowest point. Just as He reached out to Adam and Eve, Hezekiah, David, Elijah, and Peter, when you feel disappointed or defeated, the Lord Himself takes the initiative to connect with you and encourage your heart.

As you ask the Lord for His favor upon your life for the next thirty days, I am convinced that you will see wonderful breakthroughs in many areas where you seek God's blessing.

The Prayer for Salvation

Ironically, for this evangelist, the prayer for salvation was by far the most difficult chapter to write, mostly because I didn't want it to sound clichéd, biased by a North American theology. Of all the chapters, however, it is one of the most important. The reader must capture the cue and place the book into the hands of someone who can specifically benefit from it.

There are two types of salvation, the *here and now* and

the *afterlife*. In regard to the first, every human being has a hole in his or her heart that only God can fill. Unfortunately, the things that we think and do leave us wandering in a self-destructive pattern, and the consequences can have devastating effects on our bodies, relationships, families, and careers. That is why God sent Christ to bridge the gap and fill the void in our hearts and save us from ourselves.

Second, Christ came to save us from hell in the afterlife, where there is eternal torment. Those who fail to accept His redemption before their lives come to an end become completely separated from God, friends, and loved ones. There is no peace, no joy, and no rest. God values us so much that He sent His only Son to rescue us from such horror and pain.

A sincere heart that leads us to accept Christ as the way, the truth, and the life is the only necessary requirement in order to receive salvation. No matter where you find yourself in your spiritual journey, the Lord is eager to begin a relationship with you. If you have never prayed before, or if you once served Him but have fallen away, He wants to reconcile your life. God's purpose for you is not survival. It's life. And He wants you to have it more abundantly.

* * *

I want to leave this challenge with you. Take one month and lift the prayers mentioned in the pages of this book before the Lord or put them in your own words. I am convinced that after thirty days, you will see powerful and miraculous breakthroughs in your life. My prayer is that the Lord God Almighty will richly bless your life in every way.

Please use the template directions in the following section of this book to begin a prayer journal. Or you can download it from our website: TheSevenPrayers.com.

In each chapter, I have included prayers that are taken from different places in the Bible. As we conclude this book together, I would like the opportunity to pray God's blessings upon your life. Each day, before I started writing this book, I prayed for you. I trust that these pages will greatly encourage you and serve to spark a quantum leap in every area of your life!

Lord, I thank You for the wonderful life that holds this book in his or her hands. I ask that You would grant every rich blessing mentioned in these pages to this wonderful friend who diligently seeks Your help at this time. Guide at every intersection. Forgive every mistake and shortcoming. Deliver my friend from temptation, evil, vices, and all the attacks of the enemy.

I ask that You would provide for every basic need and financial challenge. Create open doors and new opportunities. Heal every sickness, and cover my friend's body, soul, and spirit with Your grace and powerful presence. May You open the floodgates of heaven and pour out such overwhelming blessing that my friend would not be able to contain it. Finally, I ask that Your salvation would permeate this life now and in the afterlife. Bless this person and his or her family for a thousand generations! I ask this in Your precious and holy name, Christ Jesus. Amen.

Instructions for a Prayer Journal

❧

"Ask and it will be given to you; seek and you will find; knock and the door will be opened to you" (Matt. 7:7).

God cares deeply about our lives and wants to help us experience powerful breakthroughs. Take a few moments and write down the issues you are facing and allow the Lord to answer your prayers over the course of the days, weeks, and months that follow. Here is a simple way to put together an effective prayer journal.

At the top left-hand side of a piece of paper, write "Date." About half an inch to the right, write "Prayer Request." Then, about four inches from the right side of the paper, write "Date Answered." On the right side, put the words "Brief Description." Then, under each of the four headings, begin to fill in your different prayer requests. Make sure that you diligently look for God's answers in the many ways He may choose to answer your prayers. Here is an example:

Date	Prayer Request	Date Answered	Brief Description
Jan. 14	We need God's guidance for choosing a school for our kids.	Jan. 21	After the interview, we knew!
Jan. 27	Car broke down and we need an alternative mode of transp.	Jan. 29	John lent us his car.
Feb. 05	Jennifer has a fever of 104. Dr isn't sure of the cause.	Feb. 06	12 hours later, fever broke!!

If you would like a free PDF template of a prayer journal with Bible verses, visit my website: TheSevenPrayers.com.

Also, if you would like me to pray for you, please visit TheSevenPrayers.com. Or in Spanish, you can visit: LasSiete Oraciones.com. There, you can leave me your petition and know that hundreds of people will lift up your request before the Lord. I want you to experience the joy of seeing God's hand work in your life!

Questions for Personal Reflection and Group Discussion

Chapter 1: The Prayer for Direction

Even there your hand will guide me, your right hand will hold me fast. (Psalm 139:10)

Questions for Personal Reflection

1. In what ways do you feel stuck?
2. What are some of your greatest frustrations?
3. In what areas do you need God's guidance?

Questions for Group Discussion

1. How does God show you His direction?
2. In what area have you experienced a breakthrough?
3. How can others pray for God's direction in your life?

Chapter 2: The Prayer for Forgiveness

For the sake of your name, O LORD, forgive my iniquity, though it is great. (Psalm 25:11)

Questions for Personal Reflection

1. In what ways do you feel you have sinned?
2. How has God's forgiveness helped you overcome that which has held you back?
3. How can you remember that God loves you in spite of your spiritual mistakes?

Questions for Group Discussion

1. In your opinion, what are the most common areas where people continue to fall short?
2. Why do some offenses stay with us a lifetime while others are easily dismissed?
3. How can your friends pray for strength and encouragement for you?

Chapter 3: The Prayer for Freedom

Rescue me and deliver me in your righteousness; turn your ear to me and save me. (Psalm 71:2)

Questions for Personal Reflection

1. In what ways do you feel oppressed?

2. In what areas do you need the power of God to set you free?
3. In chapter 3, what story do you identify with the most? Why?

Questions for Group Discussion

1. How do anger and lack of forgiveness lead to oppression?
2. How do people become slaves to addictions and vices? What impact does that have on their families?
3. In what way would you like others to pray for you so you can experience freedom?

Chapter 4: The Prayer for Provision

He directed the people to sit down on the grass. Taking the five loaves and the two fish and looking up to heaven, he gave thanks and broke the loaves. Then he gave them to the disciples, and the disciples gave them to the people. They all ate and were satisfied, and the disciples picked up twelve basketfuls of broken pieces that were left over. (Matthew 14:19–20)

Questions for Personal Reflection

1. What keeps you from falling asleep at night?
2. If you could snap your fingers and make three things happen immediately, what would you make happen?

3. How have you experienced God's provision in your life?

Questions for Group Discussion

1. In what ways do the worries you face rob you of the peace God wants you to experience?
2. What are the areas where you need God's provision?
3. How can others pray for God's provision upon your life?

Chapter 5: The Prayer for Healing

He had healed many, so that those with diseases were pushing forward to touch him. (Mark 3:10)

Questions for Personal Reflection

1. In what ways do you need God's healing in your life?
2. Have you seen or experienced healing?
3. Is there a physical, psychological, or spiritual ailment you face for which you have no solution? If so, what is it?

Questions for Group Discussion

1. In what ways can physical sickness wear down our spiritual and psychological health?
2. How does God heal us spiritually?

QUESTIONS FOR PERSONAL REFLECTION AND GROUP DISCUSSION

3. How can others pray for your physical recovery, psychological health, and spiritual redemption?

Chapter 6: The Prayer for Blessing

Surely, O LORD, you bless the righteous; you surround them with your favor as with a shield. (Psalm 5:12)

Questions for Personal Reflection

1. In what ways would you like to see the blessings of God passed onto the generations that follow you?
2. Is there a generational destructive pattern you would like to break? If so, what is it?
3. Can you identify something you are doing that is holding back God's blessings for your life?
4. Why is it difficult to believe that God wants to bless you in many ways?
5. Name three areas where you would like to see the blessings of God overflow in your life this year.

Questions for Group Discussion

1. What are some of the ways families pass on generational patterns of destruction to their children?
2. What are some of the promises and blessings of God for those who trust in the Lord? What do you *really* believe about the character of God? Will He give these wonderful things to you?

QUESTIONS FOR PERSONAL REFLECTION AND GROUP DISCUSSION

3. What are some of the blessings you want to experience in the coming months?
4. How can others pray specifically for you to experience a wonderful breakthrough?

Chapter 7: The Prayer for Salvation

Work hard for sin your whole life and your pension is death. But God's gift is *real life*, eternal life, delivered by Jesus, our Master. (Romans 6:23 MESSAGE)

Questions for Personal Reflection

1. What does God save us from in this life and in the afterlife?
2. Can you describe the hole in your heart? What seems to be missing in your life?
3. If you were to die today, would you be at peace with God? Do you have the certainty that you would enter into eternity in good standing with Him?

Questions for Group Discussion

1. What are some of the things people do to avoid beginning a relationship with God?
2. What has God done on our behalf to redeem us from a life and afterlife of destruction?
3. Would you like to begin a relationship with Christ? If so, who can you ask to join with you in prayer?

Notes

Chapter 1: The Prayer for Direction

1. See http://www.creditcards.com/credit-card-news/credit-card-industry-facts-personal-debt-statistics-1276.php.

Chapter 2: The Prayer for Forgiveness

1. See http://www.troubledteens.com/troubled-teens-statistics.html. More than 40 percent of marriages experience some sort of adulterous affair, http://www.renewamerica.com/columns/tabor/050922.
2. See http://en.wikipedia.org/wiki/Juvenile_delinquency.

Chapter 3: The Prayer for Freedom

1. F. F. Bruce, *New International Commentary on the New Testament: The Book of Acts* (Grand Rapids: Eerdmans, 1988), 105.

Chapter 4: The Prayer for Provision

1. See http://upload.wikimedia.org/wikipedia/commons/6/60/ Maslow%27s_ Hierarchy_of_Needs.svg.
2. Story paraphrased from Leon Morris, *New International Commentary on the New Testament: The Gospel of John* (Grand Rapids: Eerdmans, 1971), 489–93; and Lyle Eslinger, *The Wooing of the Woman at the Well* (New York: Oxford University Press, 1987), in *Journal of Literature and Theology* 1, 167–83.
3. Norval Geldenhuys, *New International Commentary on the New Testament: The Gospel of Luke* (Grand Rapids: Eerdmans, 1983), 182.
4. Ibid.

Chapter 5: The Prayer for Healing

1. Leon Morris, *New International Commentary on the New Testament: The Gospel of John* (Grand Rapids: Eerdmans, 1971), 299–307.
2. William Lane, *New International Commentary on the New Testament: The Gospel of Mark* (Grand Rapids: Eerdmans, 1974), 192.

Chapter 6: The Prayer for Blessing

1. See http://en.wikipedia.org/wiki/Greek_drachma.
2. Leon Morris, *New International Commentary on the New Testament: The Gospel of John* (Grand Rapids: Eerdmans, 1971), 489–93.

Chapter 7: The Prayer for Salvation

1. Norval Geldenhuys, *New International Commentary on the New Testament: The Gospel of Luke* (Grand Rapids: Eerdmans, 1983), 470.